# Freedom Summer

## The 1964 Struggle for Civil Rights in Mississippi

SUSAN GOLDMAN RUBIN

Holiday House / New York

Text copyright © 2014 by Susan Goldman Rubin
Maps on pages 13 and 18 by Tim Wallace. Copyright © 2014 by Holiday House, Inc.
Picture credits appear on page 116. The publisher apologizes for any unintentional omissions and
will be pleased to correct any inadvertent errors or omissions in future editions.
Printed and Bound in August 2015 at Tien Wah Press, Johor Bahru, Johor Malaysia.
www.holidayhouse.com

3   5   7   9   10   8   6   4   2

Library of Congress Cataloging-in-Publication Data
Rubin, Susan Goldman.
Freedom Summer : the 1964 Struggle for Civil Rights in Mississippi / by Susan Rubin. — First Edition.
pages cm.
ISBN 978-0-8234-2920-2 (hardcover)
1. Mississippi Freedom Project—Juvenile literature. 2. Civil rights movements—Mississippi—History—
20th century—Juvenile literature. 3. Civil rights workers—Mississippi—History—20th century—Juvenile literature.
4. African Americans—Civil rights—Mississippi—History—20th century—Juvenile literature. 5. African Americans—
Suffrage—Mississippi—History—20th century—Juvenile literature. I. Title.
E185.93.M6R83 2014
323.1196'073076209046—dc23
2013020208
ISBN 978-0-8234-3557-9 (paperback)
Grateful acknowledgment is made for permission to reprint excerpts
from the following copyrighted works:

Freedom Summer by Sally Belfrage. Copyright © 1965 by Sally Belfrage.
Used by permission of the University of Virginia Press.

Freedom Summer by Bruce Watson. Copyright © by Bruce Watson, 2010.
Used by permission of the Penguin Group (USA) Inc.

Excerpts from Letters from Mississippi, edited by Elizabeth Sutherland Martínez, pp. 217-218.
Original edition copyright © 1965 and renewed 1993 by Elizabeth Sutherland Martínez.
New edition copyright © 2002 by Elizabeth Sutherland Martínez. Reprinted
with the permission of The Permissions Company, Inc. on behalf
of Zephyr Press, www.zephyrpress.org.

Stranger at the Gates by Tracy Sugarman. Copyright © 1966 by Tracy Sugarman.
Used by permission of the family and estate of Tracy Sugarman, with thanks
to David Wilk of Booktrix, Easton Studio Press, LLC.

Three Lives for Mississippi by William Bradford Huie. Copyright © 2000
by William Bradford Huie. Used by permission of Mrs. Martha Huie.

We Are Not Afraid by Seth Cagin. Copyright © April 26, 2006 by Seth Cagin.
Reprinted by permission of Nation Books,
a member of the Perseus Books Group.

We Had Sneakers, They Had Guns by Tracy Sugarman.
Copyright © 2009 by Tracy Sugarman. Used by permission of
the family and estate of Tracy Sugarman.

*To the memory of Mrs. Fannie Lou Hamer*
*and those she led in the fight*
*for freedom*

*Mrs. Hamer and friends*

*Palmer's Crossing community center*

# CONTENTS

*Charles McLaurin with summer volunteers. "Nonviolence is a weapon."*

# Acknowledgments

I am enormously grateful to Rita Schwerner Bender for granting me an interview and reminding me about what was important to tell young readers.

When I began research I turned to my alma mater, Oberlin College, and I contacted grads who had been Freedom Summer volunteers. I am indebted to Matthew Rinaldi, Linda Davis, Martha Honey, Vicki Halper, and Dave Owen, and to EJ Dickson, who had just published "Memories of a Movement" in the *Oberlin Alumni Magazine*.

Many former volunteers generously shared their recollections, photographs, and letters. I am deeply grateful to Andy Schiffrin, Leonard Edwards, Allen Reich, Mel Canal, Fred Bright Winn, Mark Levy, Donna Garde, and Allen Cooper. Special thanks to my brother-in-law Steve Rubin for putting me in touch with Andy Schiffrin.

One of the most important parts of my research was a trip to Mississippi. Words are inadequate to express my thanks to the following people who welcomed and enlightened me: Dr. Stacy White, Charles McLaurin, Dr. Leslie McLemore, Margaret Kibbee, Rev. McKinley Mack Jr., Dr. Eunice Jenkins-Palmer, Mr. Madison Shannon Palmer, Mr. Foster King, Brittany Davis, Ms. Hattie R. Jordan, and Becca Basset. At the Mississippi Department of Archives and History in Jackson, I want to thank Mr. Clarence Hunter and Ms. Minnie Watson. I also thank Dr. Eugene Giles, Mrs. Mable Giles Whitaker, and Preston Hughes for their phone interviews.

I was privileged to speak with Tracy Sugarman shortly before he passed away, and I am grateful to his wife, Gloria, daughter, Laurie Sugarman-Whittier and son, Richard Sugarman, for enabling me to present his art in this book.

I thank my editor, Mary Cash, for seeing this project through and working closely with me. I want to thank the entire team at Holiday House, especially Kelly Loughman for her invaluable assistance, designer Claire Counihan, and our publisher, John Briggs.

I'm especially indebted to Stacey Holman for helping me with photo research, and to Ben Rhodes and Hal Sadler at the General Board of Global Ministries, The United Methodist Church.

For guidance and encouragement, I thank my agent and friend George Nicholson and his assistant Caitlin McDonald. A big bouquet of gratitude to my son Andrew Rubin for his technical assistance. And to my writer friends, a huge thank-you for critiques and support. Finally, I thank my husband, Michael B. Rubin, for caring deeply about this project and cheering me on.

*Mrs. Hamer marching in Hattiesburg*

**"All we want is a chance to be part of America."**
**—Fannie Lou Hamer**

# INTRODUCTION

Fannie Lou Hamer, the youngest of twenty children and the granddaughter of slaves, had left school after sixth grade. Like most black children in the Delta she had hoed cotton in the fields to help support her family, and was able to go to school only for a few months at a time. But she loved reading. She'd pick up newspapers and pieces of magazine on the road "just to have something—anything—in print to read." However, there were some facts she didn't find out until she was forty-four.

"I had never heard, until 1962, that black people could register and vote," she said. "I'd never heard that that was in the Constitution." Mrs. Hamer attended a civil rights meeting with a friend and learned that if she had a chance to vote she could vote out "hateful policemen" who had terrorized her community.

Twice she tried to register to vote in Sunflower County, Mississippi. As a result she lost her home and her job. Even worse, she was jailed and beaten, and her life was threatened. "Well, killing or no killing," she said, "I'm going to stick with civil rights." Her spirit and way of inspiring people, and her affecting speeches and rousing songs, caught the attention of organizers in the civil rights movement. One organization, the Student Nonviolent Coordinating Committee (SNCC), recruited her to be a leader. In the early 1960s SNCC and other civil rights groups were working to empower black people through the vote. In a letter to Northern supporters Mrs. Hamer wrote, "I am determined to become a first class citizen. . . . I am determined to get every Negro in the State of Mississippi registered."

This was the beginning of Freedom Summer.

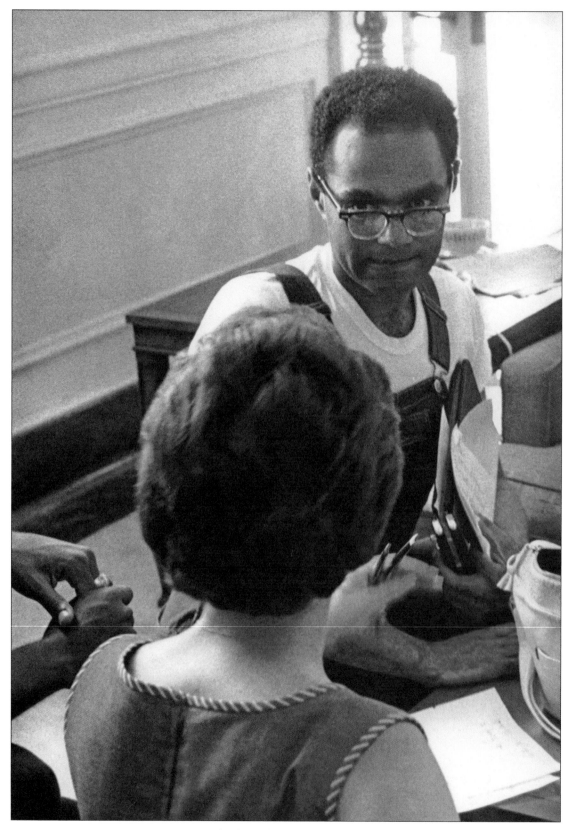

*SNCC leader Bob Moses, Oxford, Ohio*

# CHAPTER ONE
# June 1964

On the morning of June 13, 1964, Andrew Goodman hugged and kissed his mother good-bye and "went off to fight for freedom."

"I'm scared," he told a friend. "I'm scared but I'm going."

That night Andrew, age twenty, arrived at Western College for Women in Oxford, Ohio, to begin a week of orientation with 250 other college students. He had volunteered to take part in the Mississippi Summer Project, also known as Freedom Summer. A number of major civil rights groups had joined forces to form the Council of Federated Organizations (COFO) to confront bigotry in Mississippi.

The project would be dangerous. Racism was rampant everywhere but particularly overt in the South, and especially strong in Mississippi. The plan was to bring Northern college students like Andrew into Mississippi to try to register blacks to vote, and to establish Freedom Schools where blacks could be prepared to register and learn about their history and constitutional rights. At that time only 6.4 percent of eligible blacks in Mississippi were registered voters, even though blacks made up more than half the state's population. White supremacists who ran the government and businesses wanted to keep things just as they were. Blacks who tried to register to vote had experiences like those of Mrs. Hamer. They were beaten, tortured, and some were murdered.

"This is terrible," Andrew said to his parents when he announced that he had applied for the program. "We're living in what is supposed to be a democracy, and they're not allowed to vote. If someone says he cares about people, how can he not be concerned about this?"

His parents worried about his safety. Volunteers under the age of twenty-one needed their parents' permission after they successfully completed the application process. Every volunteer received a memo saying, "We hope you

*Questions from the Mississippi Summer Project application for volunteers, 1964*

are making preparations to have bond money ready in the event of your arrest. Bond money for a single arrest usually runs around $500."

It was as though Andrew were going off to fight in a war. When he left for the training program his mother slipped iodine and bandages into his duffel bag in case he was hurt.

The Summer Project had been initiated by a newly formed civil rights organization called the Student Nonviolent Coordinating Committee (SNCC, pronounced "Snick"). Other organizations participated as part of the Council of Federated Organizations (COFO): the Congress of Racial Equality (CORE), the National Association for the Advancement of Colored People (NAACP), and the Southern Christian Leadership Council (SCLC). The leaders knew that the college volunteers might be beaten and injured. But they also realized that violence could draw national attention to the brutality and lawlessness in Mississippi that blacks had been suffering for decades. At planning meetings some staffers opposed the idea of bringing in white volunteers. Yet older local people almost unanimously approved and saw the program as something positive that could finally bring real change to Mississippi.

*An excerpt from Bob Moses's memo to accepted applicants regarding bond money, 1964*

On Sunday, June 14, 1964, the first day of orientation in Ohio, Andrew and the other volunteers had ID pictures taken. Each held a number under his or her chin and sat for two poses. After dinner volunteers enthusiastically strummed guitars and sang freedom songs. Arms crossed, they swayed and belted out "We Shall Overcome." At some point during the week Mrs. Hamer arrived straight from a speaking engagement to help with the training, and led the group in singing what became her signature anthem:

*Singing during orientation led by Chuck Neblett, a SNCC Freedom Singer, and Mrs. Hamer*

> *This little light of mine,*
> *I'm gonna let it shine.*

But on the first night Bob Moses, the director of the Summer Project, took the stage. Moses, a slender black man, wore the uniform of SNCC staffers: blue denim overalls and a white T-shirt. He had earned a master's degree in philosophy at Harvard and had taught at a prestigious private school in New York City, but had given up teaching to work in the South for the civil rights movement.

"The quiet grace of him compelled you to watch," wrote Tracy Sugarman, an artist and veteran of World War II who had come to participate and record what he observed.

In a low voice Moses told the kids that the aim of the project was to get the federal government to intervene in Mississippi. "This is part of what we are doing," he said, "getting the country involved through yourselves. Don't come to Mississippi this summer to save the Mississippi Negro. Only come if you understand, really understand, that his freedom and yours are one."

Mississippi had been called "the Closed Society," Moses said. "It is closed, locked. We think the key is the vote."

Andrew and the others were warned that they would face hostility, and that whites in Mississippi would regard them as troublemakers, intruders, "race-mixing *trash*." The volunteers had much to learn in only a week: How to avoid being beaten or killed. How to talk to a group of threatening whites. How not to dress. How to cope with tear gas.

They received SNCC security handbooks that read, "No one should go *anywhere* alone, but certainly not in an automobile and certainly not at

*A portion of a memo to accepted applicants giving current information on growing expectations of hostility in Mississippi, June 11, 1964 (See Appendix A)*

night. . . . Travel at night should be avoided unless absolutely necessary. . . . Try not to sleep near open windows. . . . Try to sleep at the back of the house."

They were told to listen for an accelerating car outside any building in which they were working or staying. That might signal that a firebomb had been thrown. In Mississippi the police were *not* their friends as they had been taught as children in the North, it was explained. The volunteers had to realize that things were different in the South. Many students were appropriately scared. One leader told them, "If you don't get scared pack up and get the hell out of here, because we don't need any people who don't know what they're doing." A few recruits dropped out, but Andrew stayed.

On Monday morning Andrew registered and was assigned to work as a teacher in Vicksburg, Mississippi. Then classes and training sessions began.

"You must understand that nonviolence is essential to our program this summer," a staffer instructed.

In an outdoor workshop Andrew and the volunteers learned how to take a beating. They were instructed to fall, curl up in a ball, and absorb the blows. "Your legs, your thighs, your buttocks, your kidney, your back can take a kick or a billy club," said the staffer. "So can your arms and your hands. Your head can't. Your neck can't. Your groin can't."

The volunteers were divided into groups for role-playing. Andrew and some others took the part of "the mob" that was trying to prevent registrants from going into a courthouse. They were told to curse and be as brutal as possible.

One student remembered that Andrew seemed to lose himself shouting and screaming, then looked slightly "sheepish" at the anger he had displayed. Andrew had studied drama in college and got caught up in his part. But the

instructors said that the scene enacted by the recruits was nothing compared to what might really happen once they were in Mississippi.

Charles McLaurin, a young SNCC staffer from Jackson, Mississippi, who wore dark glasses, conducted a workshop on Sunflower County, where he had been working. Many years later he said, "I started wearing dark glasses to mask the fear they [white attackers] might see in my eyes. Once I knew my mission I did that. Sometimes I'd be put in jail." He had been the one whom Bob Moses had sent to recruit Mrs. Hamer in 1962, and he had brought her to a SNCC leadership meeting at Tougaloo College in Jackson. That night at the meeting she had told her story and sang, and, McLaurin said, SNCC "fell in love with Fannie Lou Hamer" and put her on the staff as a field secretary.

Now McLaurin told the volunteers how he had been in jail just two weeks before the training session began. He and five other SNCC staff workers had been forced off the road by the Mississippi Highway Patrol as they were driving to a meeting in Atlanta, Georgia. They were arrested without a charge, held "for investigation," then badly beaten. McLaurin's back tooth was still loose and his mouth "was a mess."

The week of training attracted national attention, and the campus swarmed with reporters and photographers. A photographer for *Look* magazine, a popular biweekly of the time that was famous for its photographs, included pictures of McLaurin talking to volunteers for an article titled "Mississippi, the Attack on Bigotry."

*Charles McLaurin leads the first meeting in Williams Chapel.*

"*Look* magazine is searching for the ideal naïve Northern middle-class white girl," a volunteer wrote to his family. "For the national press, that's the big story. And when one of us gets killed, the story will be even bigger."

On June 16 three experienced Mississippi civil rights field workers arrived to help train the volunteers. They were Michael Henry Schwerner, nicknamed Mickey; his wife, Rita; and their friend James Earl Chaney. Mickey, age twenty-four, and Rita, twenty-two, had been working in Meridian, Mississippi, for CORE. They had turned a dirty old office into a Freedom House with a library, and it had become a thriving community center.

Mickey was a professional social worker who had worked with teens in New York City. Rita was a teacher. But in Meridian they had aroused anger among the whites because they were outsiders, Jews, and "mixers." Members of the Ku Klux Klan, a group of white supremacists dedicated to preserving segregation, were particularly active in Mississippi. Local members hated Mickey's beatnik appearance. He had a goatee and always wore a sweatshirt, jeans, and sneakers. Mickey's beard particularly offended Klansmen, and they sneeringly called him "Goatee" and "Whiskers."

Mickey didn't let insults from the Klan stop his efforts. He wanted to work with the Negro community, and had recruited assistants for his projects from high-school- and college-age Negroes. James Chaney, a twenty-one-year-old high-school dropout and a native of Meridian, volunteered to help. James worked hard "building shelves, loading books, painting," wrote Mickey and Rita in a letter to the national CORE office. He and Mickey became close friends, and Mickey had him officially appointed to the staff. CORE provided the staff with a blue Ford station wagon that had probably been a gift from black actor Sydney Poitier. James was a deft driver and knew all the back roads in the area. At night he could speed down dirt tracks and through rural areas with the headlights off to avoid detection by the Ku Klux Klan. James traveled through Mississippi, stopping at shacks to talk to black families who were brave enough to risk being seen speaking to the civil rights workers and accepting voting leaflets.

In June, James, Mickey, and Rita had driven together to Oxford, Ohio, for the Summer Project training, and there they met Andrew Goodman.

"All of us were delighted with him," said Rita. "He was such a fine, intelligent, unassuming young man. He and I had much to talk about because he was a student at my alma mater, Queens College."

Mickey also had a lot in common with Andrew. They both came from Jewish families in New York and cared deeply about the civil rights movement. Andrew told Mickey about some of the demonstrations he had participated in, and papers he had written in college, and Mickey was impressed.

He asked Andrew if he would like to work in Meridian instead of teaching in Vicksburg.

Meanwhile another civil rights worker on the staff, Eric Weinberger, also invited Andrew to work with him that summer. Weinberger and his wife, Elaine, were going to organize a cooperative in Canton, Mississippi, modeled after a successful program they had run in Tennessee. There they had started a leatherworking project among black sharecroppers who had been evicted from their homes for registering to vote. The cooperative made "Tote Bags for Integration."

Andrew was flattered by the two invitations. He decided to go to Canton with Weinberger, and called his mother to tell her about the change in plans.

That same day Mickey received alarming and sad news.

Mount Zion Methodist Church in Neshoba County, where the community planned to provide a place for a Freedom School, had been burned down. There had been a meeting at the church and members of the Ku Klux Klan mistakenly thought it was a political freedom meeting at which they could find Mickey. The Klan planned to get rid of Mickey to intimidate the Negroes from voting, and to "scare the Commie college students who are thinking about coming to Mississippi."

But Mickey was in Oxford, Ohio, at the time of the incident. And the black church members were merely holding a meeting to discuss business and money matters.

A mob of white men from Meridian had waited for the congregation members as they left the church that night, and blocked the road in both directions. "Where's the Jew-boy with the beard?" they demanded as they searched the cars. When they didn't find Mickey they beat some of the church members, breaking one woman's collarbone. Later a few of the attackers returned to Mount Zion Methodist Church and burned it to the ground.

When Mickey heard the news the next day, he wanted to return to Mississippi immediately and build a Freedom School on the site of the burned church. Once again he asked Andrew to go with him. He needed a particularly effective volunteer as an assistant to do community organizing. Andrew accepted the offer and on Friday night called his parents to tell them the news. "Don't worry," he said. "I'm going to a CORE area. It's safer."

Rita wanted to go back to Mississippi with Mickey, but he urged her to stay in Oxford and help train the second group of volunteers, who were due to arrive that weekend.

At 3 a.m. on Saturday, June 20, Andrew, Mickey, James, and five other volunteers—Andy Schiffrin, Louise Hermey, David Cotz, John Stevenson, and Edna Perkins—piled into the blue Ford station wagon and drove off to Mississippi. They needed to get to Meridian before dark.

# CHAPTER TWO

# June 20, 1964

*Mrs. Waterhouse with her daughters Rosalyn on the left, Patricia on the right, and Lelia Jean in back*

At 5:30 p.m. Andrew, Mickey, James, and the other volunteers arrived in Meridian. "Mickey did all the driving," remembered Andy Schiffrin, a sociology major who had just graduated from UCLA. He had been assigned to assist Mickey with research. "When we hit the South, Chaney had to duck down," said Schiffrin. "It was dangerous for him to be seen with civil rights activists, and a black man with a white woman was a problem."

Over supper at Beal's café in the black part of town, Mickey gave out housing assignments. Students in the Summer Project stayed with courageous local black families who risked their homes and safety by having them as guests. "I stayed with the Waterhouse family," said Schiffrin, and he quickly became friends with the Waterhouse daughters: Lelia Jean, Rosalyn, and Patricia.

The first black person who hosted white volunteers was Mrs. Irene Magruder in Indianola. "Her opening her door to us was very, very brave," said Fred Bright Winn, one of the volunteers who stayed with her. "She opened her door to us because she had seen a lifetime of wrong and she wanted to change it." Feisty and independent, Mrs. Magruder dipped snuff, made quilts, raised and killed her own chickens, and had started the White Rose Cafe where volunteers went to eat spicy hamburgers and pigs' feet. Mrs. Magruder's decision encouraged others to risk taking in volunteers. "But because of her choice," said Winn, "her house was firebombed nine months later."

Since Andrew had decided to go to Meridian at the last minute, no housing arrangements had been made for him. Temporarily he would stay at Mickey and Rita's apartment.

After supper Mickey, James, and Andrew dropped off the other volunteers with their host families, and they went to James's house. James, one of five children, lived with his mother, Mrs. Fannie Lee Chaney. A wonderful baker, she had made a lemon pie for Mickey and had brought home doughnuts from the bakery where she worked. As they feasted Andrew talked with James's twelve-year-old brother, Ben, who was interested in the civil rights movement. Then the three young men decided to go to the movies.

In Meridian the movie theaters, like everything else at that time, were segregated, so they went to a Negro theater and saw a horror film. When James got home around midnight, his mother was waiting up for him. He told her about his experiences in Oxford, Ohio. It was the first time he had ever been up north. Excitedly he said that many more civil rights workers would be arriving the next day. As James kissed his mother good night, he urged, "Mom, cook up lots of food tomorrow. All the students are coming over."

On Sunday morning, June 21, James's mother fixed breakfast for him and his coworkers. When they left the house Ben begged to go along. James refused, but promised to take Ben driving when he got back that afternoon.

At the Meridian community center the trio

*Mrs. Magruder in front of the remains of her fire-bombed house in Indianola*

*Ben Chaney
and volunteer
Mel Canal in
Meridian*

reviewed their travel plans with Sue Brown, a black high-school senior who had been volunteering at the center, and with Andy Schiffrin and Louise Hermey. Louise was put in charge of "communication" and helped man the phone. Mickey told Sue they would be driving to Longdale, in Neshoba County, to inspect what was left of the burned-down Mount Zion Church and to visit the church members who had been beaten. In the months Mickey had been working in Mississippi he had received many threatening phone calls, and was well aware that going to the scene of the crime so soon after the fire was dangerous. However, he felt responsible for the attack. He had been the one to persuade the congregation to let him open a Freedom School at their church.

There was an unbreakable rule for SNCC workers: Whenever they traveled anywhere they were to let staff members know precisely where they were going and what time they would return. If a group was not back by the specified time, the staffer would start making emergency calls. Two WATS (Wide Area Telephone Service) lines had been set up for that purpose. One line was national, the other was state, and they were manned around the clock by civil rights workers.

Mickey told Sue he expected to be back at the community center by 4 p.m. She said, "If you're not back by four, what time do I start calling?"

"At four-thirty," said Mickey.

Before leaving Meridian, he and Andrew went to get their hair cut at the home of a black student barber. Andrew didn't get shaved because he had decided to grow a beard like Mickey's. It was a hot, humid morning, the temperature already close to 100, but the weather didn't seem to faze Andrew. It was Father's Day, and he sent a postcard to his parents:

Dear Mom and Dad,

I have arrived safely in Meridian, Miss. This is a wonderful town, and the weather is fine. I wish you were here. The people in this city are wonderful, and our reception was very good.

All my love,
Andy

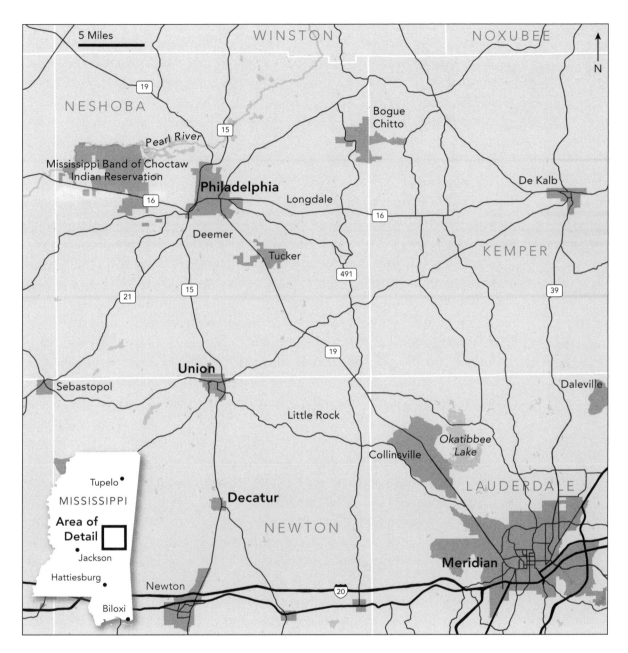

He and James had the blue Ford station wagon filled with gas at a Negro-owned station in Meridian. SNCC workers kept their cars in excellent condition. "A tire or engine failure at the wrong time and place could be fatal," Rita explained. As a precaution she and Mickey had bought new tires in April.

At noon Mickey, James, and Andrew took off for Longdale. By one o'clock they had reached the home of Ernest Kirkland. Kirkland had been one of the first blacks in Neshoba County to support the civil rights program. Although he had not been present at Mount Zion Church the night it was burned down, he went with the group to examine the site. Then they visited Cornelius Steele, who had witnessed the Klan attack. Steele took them to see Bud Cole, who had been pistol-whipped nearly to death by the Klansmen. Bud was in too much pain to stand up to greet the men. He warned Mickey that the Klan had been looking for him that night, and that the blows he had taken were meant for Mickey.

After they left the Coles', Kirkland invited the group back to his house for refreshments. Despite everything Andy had seen and heard that day, his first day in Mississippi, he still felt upbeat about spending the summer working at a Freedom School. Around 3 p.m. Mickey announced it was time to go.

The three young men left with James at the wheel of the station wagon. Instead of driving back the way they had come, on Highway 491, they seemed to have decided to take Highway 16. Most likely, they knew the Klan would be looking for them, and figured they'd be safer on Highway 16, a bigger two-lane road with more traffic. On that road it would be harder for the Klan to stage an ambush.

James, obeying the speed limit, drove at sixty-five miles an hour. Coming toward him was a 1957 Chevy sedan. The driver was Neshoba County Deputy Sheriff Cecil Ray Price, a Klansman. James carefully maintained his speed as Price roared past him. Andrew and Mickey ducked down. Whites riding with blacks infuriated the police, who often pulled over such cars "and 'investigated.'"

As James crested a hill and began the descent he noticed a police cruiser parked under a shade tree on the side of the road. Two patrolmen were sitting there waiting to catch speeding cars. James continued to drive at sixty-five as he approached the town of Philadelphia.

All of a sudden James spotted Price's Chevy in his rearview mirror. He was tempted to floor the gas pedal and make a run for it. But James realized that he wouldn't be able to outrun Price through Philadelphia, where the speed limit was thirty-five miles an hour. Price turned on his red police light and honked, signaling James to stop. A CORE staffer had instructed James never to stop for a white policeman. However, at that moment one of the new tires went flat, and James pulled over.

# CHAPTER THREE

# June 21, 1964, afternoon

Deputy Price got out of his car and ordered James, Mickey, and Andrew to change the tire before he took them to jail. He was arresting James for speeding, and charging Mickey and Andy as suspects in the firebombing of Mount Zion Church. Price radioed the two patrolmen, E. R. Poe and Harry J. Wiggs, to come and assist him in taking the prisoners to jail. Wiggs drove the station wagon with James as his passenger, and Mickey and Andrew climbed into the backseat of Poe's patrol car. Because of the heat, Poe had taken off his leather gun belt and left it lying on the back seat. When Poe turned around to get it, Mickey handed it to him. Later Poe said, "I guess that's the first time a prisoner ever handed me my own gun."

With Price in the lead, the cars reached the Neshoba County jail at about 4 p.m. The one-story brick building was operated by a white couple, Mr. and Mrs. Herring. Price told Mrs. Herring to book James for speeding, and to hold Mickey and Andrew "for investigation." Mrs. Herring took the young men's driving licenses and wallets. Mickey asked Price if he could make a phone call and was told no.

Price wanted all three civil rights workers to be locked up together in the same cell. However, Mr. Herring insisted on keeping his jail segregated. So Mickey and Andrew were put in a cell with Billy Charles McKay, another white prisoner, and James was led to a cell in the back that was occupied by Cotton Roosevelt, a young black man.

By 4:20 p.m. Mickey asked again if he could make a phone call. He knew that Sue Brown would be anxious. Unbeknownst to Mickey, calls were already being made to check on his whereabouts. Louise Hermey, who was manning the phone at the Meridian community center, called COFO headquarters in Jackson to express her concern that Mickey, Andrew, and

James hadn't returned or checked in. She was told to wait an hour, the three men might have had car trouble.

At 4:45 Mickey appealed to his jailer, Mr. Herring, as a married man, to let him call his wife. Herring softened and offered to call Mickey's wife for him. Mickey was in a jam since Rita was in Oxford, Ohio, hundreds of miles away. If Herring called the community center and asked for her, he might discover that Mickey had tricked him. More importantly, if Herring called for him Mickey probably realized he was giving up the right he believed he had to a phone call. Furthermore, he wouldn't have been able to trust what Herring might say on his behalf. So Mickey declined the jailer's offer.

At 5:30 one of the jailers took a phone call from COFO inquiring whether Mickey, James, and Andrew were there or had been seen. Whoever answered the phone denied any knowledge of the three young men.

Mrs. Herring fixed supper for the prisoners, a typical Southern meal: chicken and dumplings, green beans, corn bread, cake, and iced tea. Andrew and Mickey devoured the food hungrily. Afterward they relaxed a little. Their cellmate, McKay, said they seemed "calm and collected." The young men expected to be held a few days till court would be in session and their case could be heard.

But at 10 p.m. Price came to the jail and said he would release them if James paid the twenty-dollar fine for speeding. Price unlocked their cells and led them into the jail office. Mrs. Herring returned their driver's licenses and wallets, and Mickey paid the fine.

According to Mrs. Herring's trial testimony, Price said to them, "Now, let's see how quick y'all can get out of Neshoba County."

He escorted them to a vacant lot near the jail where their station wagon was parked. Rita and other people who worked at Meridian with Mickey later said that he must have wanted to make a phone call perhaps from the phone booth in the lobby of a hotel across the street. It was a CORE rule to call the CORE office in Meridian or Jackson to report on why they were late. But they probably did not have time. Price hurried them along, and they wanted to get out of town quickly.

When they got into the station wagon, Price and Officer Richard Willis tailed them out of town to Highway 19. It is not certain who was driving, Mickey or James. They sped down the highway, undoubtedly relieved to be free. Passing a gas station, Mickey most likely considered stopping to use the pay phone. But according to later testimonies the patrolmen who had helped Price arrest them earlier were parked there. So they kept on moving.

All of a sudden Price reappeared in pursuit. As the station wagon neared the Neshoba County line, a posse of Ku Klux Klansmen in a Chevy joined the chase. James was at the wheel. He accelerated and made a run for it. The Chevy skidded to a stop on the side of the road. Another group of Klansmen roared up in a Ford sedan. James tore down the road. At the crest of a hill he swerved into Highway 492. Price followed and flipped on his red flashing light. James slowed down and stopped at the side of the road.

The Ford sedan with the Klansmen pulled up. Price, holding a black-jack, went over to the station wagon. One of the conspirators, James Jordan, overheard Price say to James, "I thought you were going back to Meridian if we let you out of jail."

"We were going there," said James.

"Well," said Price, "you sure were taking the long way around. Get out of the car."

Price ordered James, Mickey, and Andrew to get into the back of his car. When James hesitated, Price hit him over the head with his blackjack. The three young men stumbled into Price's car. Price instructed one of the white men to drive the station wagon. With Price in the lead, the three cars headed back toward Philadelphia. A few minutes later Price turned off on a dark, deserted road known locally as Rock Cut Road. The caravan of cars came to a halt and parked. The Ford kept its headlights on. By then it was almost midnight.

The men got out of their cars. One of them, Wayne Roberts, yanked Mickey out of Price's car. In the glare of the headlights and by the light of the moon he spun Mickey around and placed him at the edge of a ditch. In unison some of the Klansmen chanted, "Ashes to ashes / Dust to dust / If you stayed where you belonged / You wouldn't be here with us."

Another said, "So you wanted to come to Mississippi? Well, now we're gonna let you stay here."

Roberts held a pistol to Mickey's heart and fired. Mickey fell into the ditch.

Then Roberts pulled Andrew out of Price's car and shot him in the chest. Andrew doubled up and fell backward.

Jordan shouted, "Save one for me." As Jordan hauled James onto the road, James struggled. Recognizing one of the Klansmen from Meridian, James begged him to spare his life.

Jordan shot James in the stomach and he fell to the ground. Roberts fired, too, hitting James in the lower back; then he shot him in the head.

The murderers tossed the three bodies into the station wagon and drove along dirt roads to an unfinished dam at Old Jolly Farm. A bulldozer

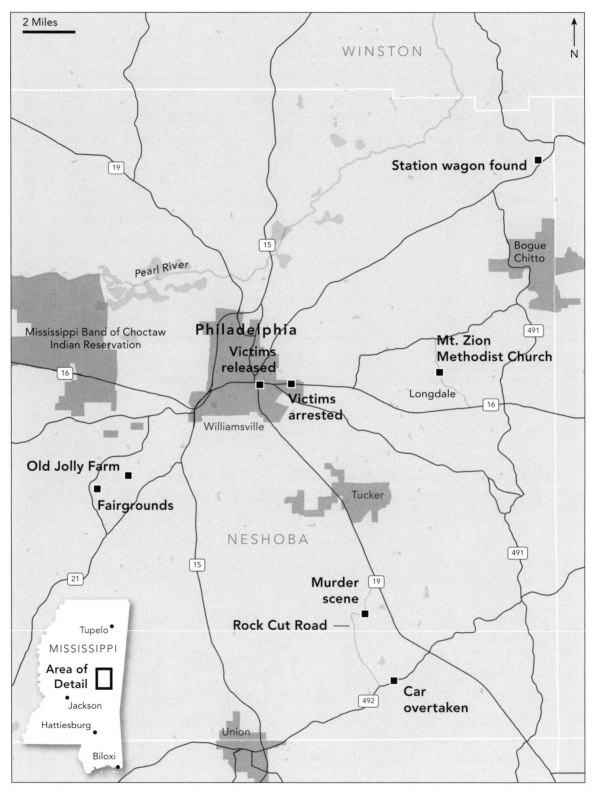

2 Miles

WINSTON

N

19

15

Pearl River

Station wagon found

Bogue
Chitto

491

Mississippi Band of Choctaw
Indian Reservation

16

Philadelphia

Victims
released

Mt. Zion
Methodist Church

Longdale

16

Victims
arrested

Williamsville

Old Jolly Farm

Fairgrounds

Tucker

NESHOBA

15

491

Murder
scene

19

Rock Cut Road

21

MISSISSIPPI

Tupelo

Area of
Detail

Jackson

Car
overtaken

492

Hattiesburg

Union

Biloxi

*Events within Neshoba County*

operator was waiting for them and dug a trench. The killers dumped the bodies, fully clothed, face down, into the red clay base of the dam and covered them with fifteen feet of dirt. Afterward they drove the blue Ford station wagon to Bogue Chitto Swamp fifteen miles northeast of Philadelphia and burned it.

Back in Philadelphia they congratulated one another for cleverly hiding the bodies and destroying the station wagon.

A state official joined them at the courthouse square and said, "Well, boys, you've done a good job. Mississippi can be proud of you. . . . Go home now and forget it. The first man who talks is *dead*!"

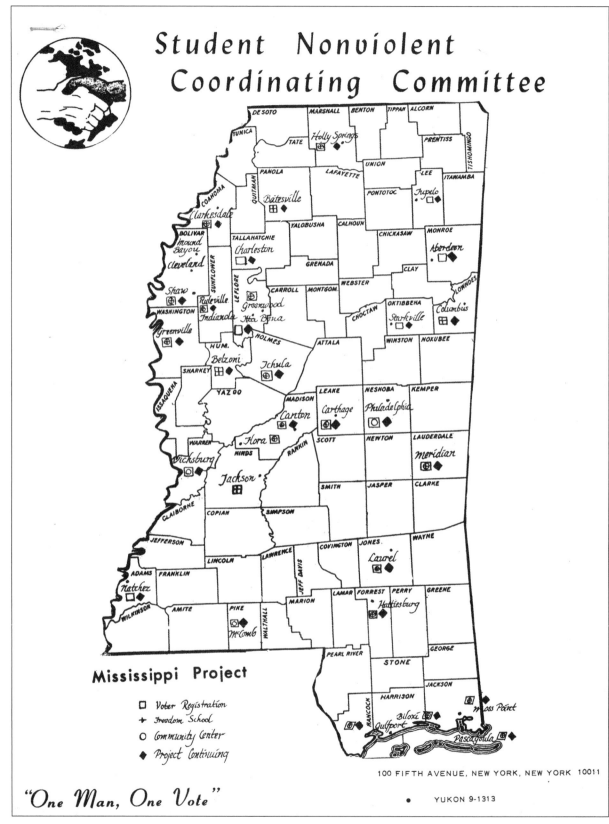

# Student Nonviolent Coordinating Committee

Mississippi Project

☐ Voter Registration
✛ Freedom School
○ Community Center
◆ Project Continuing

"One Man, One Vote"

100 FIFTH AVENUE, NEW YORK, NEW YORK 10011

• YUKON 9-1313

*A map of Freedom Summer projects from a SNCC report*

# CHAPTER FOUR

# June 22, 1964, early morning

Rita Schwerner was wakened at 1 a.m. in Oxford, Ohio. She hurried across the darkened quad to the office to accept a long-distance call from Atlanta, Georgia. Over the phone Mary King, a staff member of SNCC, told her that Mickey, James, and Andrew were missing and thought to be in jail somewhere. Rita was stunned. For the rest of the night she stayed up making calls.

She tried phoning President Lyndon B. Johnson at the White House, but a Secret Service agent refused to wake him up. The lives of three men are at stake, said Rita. If anything happens to them, the president will have to share the responsibility.

At 1:40 a.m. Mary King phoned Andrew Goodman's parents in New York and told them the news. She suggested that they contact their congressman, who might be able to start pressuring the government to look into the disappearances. The FBI would investigate only if there was proof that a federal law had been violated. The Goodmans asked Mary King to call them back immediately if there was any news.

In Meridian, Mrs. Chaney had already been told and feared the worst. Her Grandpa Jim had "disappeared" because he had stood up against white neighbors by refusing to sell his farmland to them. "I'm just hoping and not thinking," she said.

All through the night COFO workers in Meridian, Jackson, and Atlanta were desperately spreading the word that the three young men were missing. They phoned federal officials, news reporters, and prominent people to help press the government to do something. Without a sheriff's order, no missing-persons bulletin could be issued for seventy-two hours. Sheriff Lawrence Rainey, who was well known among Neshoba County blacks for his brutality, was unlikely to issue the order.

At 6:55 a.m. a staff worker making follow-up calls to all the jails and hospitals in the area once again phoned the Neshoba County Jail. Finally Mrs. Herring admitted that the three young men had been arrested on Sunday afternoon. Then she lied and said they had been released at 6 p.m. after paying a fine for speeding.

The lie was repeated by Sheriff Rainey at the Neshoba County Courthouse. Rainey confirmed Mrs. Herring's report and said that his deputy, Cecil Price, had seen the three civil rights workers poking around the wreckage of the burned Mount Zion Church and had arrested them for speeding away.

This information was relayed to Rita and the Goodmans. Rita phoned her in-laws in Pelham, New York, and broke the news that Mickey was missing. A little while later Andrew's parents called the Schwerners and discussed plans to fly to Washington, D.C., the next day if their sons had not been found.

At 9:30 that Monday morning the second group of Summer Project volunteers assembled in Oxford to begin their week of orientation. Bob Moses, the director, opened the session by explaining the purpose of the project. He did not yet know that the three young men were missing. On a blackboard he drew a map of Mississippi and discussed Klan activities in the various counties: Sunflower, Madison, Leflore, Yazoo, Neshoba . . .

"Our goals are limited," he said. "If we can go and come back alive, then that is something. If you can go into Negro homes and just sit and talk, that will be a huge job."

The three hundred students listened intently. As Moses was discussing racially motivated hatred and the role of nonviolence, a SNCC staff member took him aside. Moses looked stricken as he took in the news.

Then he stood gazing at the floor without speaking. Finally he said, "Yesterday morning, three of our people left Meridian, Mississippi, to investigate a church-burning in Neshoba County. They haven't come back, and we haven't had any word from them. We spoke to John Doar in the Justice Department. He promised to order the FBI to act, but the local FBI still says they have been given no authority."

Doar, assistant attorney general in the Justice Department's Civil Rights Division, was a friend of Moses and sympathetic to the Summer Project. However, he had told the first group of volunteers, including Andrew, that there would be no federal police protection for them in Mississippi. "The responsibility for protection is that of the local police," he said. This was the legal stance of the Johnson administration, and Doar had no power to overrule it. Angrily, the students had booed him.

Now the room buzzed with alarm. The students started talking to one another. Who were these missing people? What did it mean?

Just then Rita Schwerner walked in. She was "small physically but steadfast," remembered Martha Honey, a freshman from Oberlin College. Rita paced back and forth on the stage yet was "incredibly composed" as she told the students details about the arrest of the three civil rights workers. Martha said, "I was in awe that a wife could be that brave, that she could speak so rationally about the disappearance of her husband, Mickey." Rita believed that her husband, Andrew, and James were alive, and asked the students to help find them. She instructed them to form groups according to their home states and to wire their congressmen demanding that the federal government investigate. She explained that if the government didn't act, none of them would be safe. Someone in the audience asked her to spell the names of the three men.

Rita went to the blackboard and erased part of the map of Mississippi. She picked up a piece of chalk and in large letters wrote:

James Chaney – CORE staff
Michael Schwerner – CORE staff
Andrew Goodman – Summer Project volunteer
Neshoba County – disappeared

Everyone in the auditorium thought, *This could happen to me.*

"No one was willing to believe that the event involved more than a disappearance," remembered Sally Belfrage, a volunteer from England. "The tension clouded us in until it was all there was to breathe."

*Summer volunteer Martha Honey, from Oberlin College*

# CHAPTER FIVE
# June 22, 1964

Rita said to the volunteers, "You all have to make a decision about what you have to do. This is what you're up against."

After she finished speaking some students lined up at the pay phone to call their parents. Most broke into groups as Rita had asked, composed telegrams to their congressmen, and collected money to send them by wire.

One student wrote to her parents, "Everyone suspects the worst to have happened to the men but no one says anything."

Bob Moses left the building to sit on the steps outside, looking desolate. Friends came over to hug him, and tried to convince him that he was not responsible.

But Moses felt that he was. Freedom Summer had been mainly his idea, and he had made it happen. Moses, a SNCC veteran, had first gone to Mississippi in the early 1960s to participate in the voter registration effort, believing that with the vote blacks could take control of their lives and bring about change. When progress on voter registration stalled in 1963, Moses had thought of recruiting white volunteers to help, which would call everyone's attention to the civil rights movement. At first other members of the SNCC staff as well as COFO member organizations hotly debated Moses's plan to include white outsiders in their struggle. Finally they agreed and rallied behind the Summer Project. Moses knew there would be danger. In the spring of 1964 he had formed Friends of Freedom in Mississippi and they had written to President Lyndon B. Johnson urging federal protection for the volunteers. The president had not responded. Now Moses sat outside the auditorium, staring into space.

Meanwhile in Mississippi, at the Meridian community center, "there was such chaos," remembered Andy Schiffrin. "We were figuring out what to do." Louise Hermey took charge of the phone. Sue Brown and Charles Young, a black hotel owner and NAACP member, drove into Neshoba County looking for any trace of the missing men and their blue station wagon. Four teams of SNCC organizers including Stokely Carmichael, Charlie Cobb, and Cleveland Sellers joined in the search. During the day they slept in the homes of black sharecroppers, and dared to go out only after midnight to avoid being seen by the Klan. Local people carrying shotguns combed the woods, pretending to hunt. "We searched swamps, creeks, old houses, abandoned barns, orchards, tangled underbrush, and unused wells," said Sellers. "Our search was complicated by the poisonous snakes and spiders that abound in rural Mississippi." But their efforts were fruitless. They found nothing.

That afternoon in Oxford the students continued their training and split up to prepare for their chosen programs: Freedom Schools, community centers, and voter registration. Meanwhile CORE staffers repeated their calls to Washington, stepping up pressure. They arranged a press conference to discuss the government's inaction. Since the Senate had just passed the Civil Rights Act outlawing segregation, this was particularly bad publicity that would make the Johnson administration look hypocritical. Could the federal government be embarrassed into action?

At 5:20 p.m. a press conference began at the COFO office in Jackson. John Doar called the Atlanta CORE office with new information: The three young men had been released from jail at 10 p.m., not 6:00. They had been seen driving south on Highway 19. An FBI agent from New Orleans had interviewed the Mount Zion congregation members in Longdale who Mickey, Andrew, and James had visited on Sunday. The agent had also questioned Deputy Price and Sheriff Rainey in Philadelphia.

Price admitted to arresting the three civil rights workers. Rainey was defiant. "If they're missing," he said, "they hid somewhere, trying to get a lot of publicity out of it. . . . They're somewhere around laughing at the commotion they've stirred up." The idea that the disappearance was a hoax quickly took hold in Mississippi.

Preston Hughes, a white cadet home on leave from the U.S. Military Academy at West Point, remembered that at a family gathering in Kosciusko, near Philadelphia, the older men said, "Those boys [the three civil rights workers] are back in Chicago as a ruse to embarrass Mississippi."

The editor of the *Neshoba Democrat*, a local newspaper, said of the civil rights workers, "They'll do anything to raise money. This is just the kind of hoax they pull on us and then we get all the publicity for it."

The *Fiery Cross*, the official publication of the United Klans of America, quoted the imperial wizard, who said that the disappearance was "a hoax intended to raise more money for the civil rights movement. . . . They put weeping mothers and wives on national television and try to touch the hearts of the nation."

OFFICIAL PUBLICATION, UNITED KLANS OF AMERICA, 401 ALSTON BLDG., TUSCALOOSA, ALA.

JULY

## Telephone Recording Electrifies New Orleanians

**Rev. Ronald Melancon Tells Sacred Heart High Girls It Is Mortal Sin To Refuse To Dance, Date, Sit By Negro Boys - Okays Mongrel Marriage**

New Orleans was electrified when, on March 2, Parents and Friends of Catholic Children, a group upholding racial segregation, began to broadcast the following telephone message to anyone able to get the organization's number 242-5500:

"Parents and Friends of Catholic Children: If a priest by the name of Father Melancon of St. Francis Xavier has his way, many of your white daughters will date and marry Negro boys. For it was at a recent Assembly lecture that he told the girls of Sacred Heart High here in New Orleans that it was perfectly alright and proper for them to marry Catholic Negroes.

"Father Melancon went on to tell your white daughters that to segregate because of race is a mortal sin and that a refusal by them to date Negro boys when asked is a stain of

Metairie, La., VE 5-0964.

Since the recording, we have learned from Parents and Friends and other reliable sources that Father Melancon also told the girls of Sacred Heart High, 3222 Canal St., New Orleans, HU 2-4130, that if they boarded a bus or streetcar and did not sit by a Negro because he was a Negro, they were committing a serious (mortal) sin!

A few people who expressed incredulity over the report on Father Melancon are perhaps unaware of the fact that race mongrelization has the support of at least two Catholic groups. A story in the Nov. 18, 1963, issue of The Washington, D.C., Evening Star said:

"Full support for the right of whites and Negroes to marry was voiced yesterday by delegates attending the annual convention of the National Catholic Conference for Interracial Justice."

The article said the NCCIJ adopted a resolution calling attention "to the fact that interracial marriage is morally and theologically (biological-

laws of 20 states that prohibit interracial marriages" at the group's annual meeting in Washington, D.C. The meeting was "attended by 75 clerical and lay leaders in theology, sociology, and other fields related to marriage and family living."

There can be no doubt that Father Melancon, and the Catholic groups cited above, are going along with one of the major aims of the Communist Party. The Daily Worker, Communist paper, May 26, 1928, listed nine demands for "social and racial equality." Demand No. 4 states: "Abolition of laws forbidding inter-marriage of persons of different races."

**Klan Wizard Calls Disappearance 'Hoax'**

PHILADELPHIA, Miss. —The imperial wizard of the United Knights of the Ku Klux Klan said today the disappear-

**Physchological Warfare (Wallace)**

The Fiery Cross, *official publication, United Klans of America, July: "Klan Wizard Calls Disappearance 'Hoax'"*

But after hearing the news on television, Florence Mars, a white native of Meridian, said, "I knew the disappearance could not be a hoax." Deputy Price had made a "stupid and terrible mistake releasing them late at night in what he must have known was a dangerous situation."

A lawyer who was a friend of the Goodmans called Robert Kennedy, the U.S. attorney general, urging him to do something. At about 6 p.m. that day, Kennedy ordered a full FBI investigation under the provisions of the Lindbergh Kidnapping Act. President Johnson was alerted. The Missisippi Highway Patrol finally issued a missing-persons bulletin.

At 6:30 Walter Cronkite, anchorman for *CBS Evening News*, who was often cited as "the most trusted man in America," spoke to the nation on television. "Good evening," he said. "Three young civil rights workers disappeared in Mississippi on Sunday night near the central Mississippi town of Philadelphia." Footage was shown that had been filmed at Oxford during the week Andrew had trained, and his picture happened to be featured. This led some people in Mississippi to charge that the disappearance had to be a plot. Why else would the cameraman focus on Andrew when there were so many other students in the lecture hall?

In Meridian, Mrs. Chaney cleaned her house over and over again. She mopped the kitchen floor four or five times, washed the dishes, dried them, and washed them again. She wouldn't allow her son Ben to go out to the park to play ball. Ben said, "I can't play in the house because it's too clean. . . . If she's not cleaning she's walking. But she doesn't go anywhere. She just walks in the yard in circles around the house." As Mrs. Chaney walked, Ben heard her humming "Rock of Ages" until the sun came up.

*Walter Cronkite*

By Tuesday morning, June 23, a team of FBI agents had arrived in Neshoba County and set up headquarters at the Delphia Courts Motel.

That day Andy Schiffrin typed a letter from the Meridian community center to his parents: "As you probably have heard three of the COFO people have been missing since Sunday. I hesitate to go into the story because it probably will all be over by the time you receive this. Simply, one of the guys was the project leader. He started the community center hear [sic] about six months ago and had a tremendous success. The people are crazy about him and everyone I've seen is extremely worried. The second guy, whose nickname is Bear [James Chaney], has lived in Meridian all his life (I think). He's Negro and has an eleven year old brother who looks just like him and is called Cub. The third guy is a summer volunteer from New York [Andrew Goodman]. . . . Right now we are sitting around the office and waiting to hear any news. . . . We've spent the last two nights here. Sunday night we got no sleep. . . . (There was just complete chaos for an hour with interviews, lawyers and the FBI.)"

In Oxford, the students assembled in the auditorium for the second day of orientation. The names that Rita had written on the blackboard were still there. The day began with an announcement: "There has been no word of the three people in Neshoba. The staff met all night. When we sing 'We are not afraid,' we mean we are afraid. . . . Many of you might want to turn around now."

"Everyone in that room had to decide whether they were willing to do what they had set out to do," said Michael Lipsky, an Oberlin student.

"I knew what we were getting in for," said Martha Honey, "and I was ready for it."

"I'm more determined to go ahead," said an Indiana student. "This proves something needs to be done."

It had been arranged for Rita to fly to Meridian, and she left for the Cincinnati airport.

In New York, Mickey's father, Nathan Schwerner, Andrew's parents, Robert and Carolyn Goodman, the Goodmans' lawyer, and a reporter from the *New York Herald Tribune* boarded a plane to Washington.

Mickey's father said, "What really gripes me is that the FBI and Justice Department took so long to get into this. . . . I haven't slept three hours since Sunday."

The group was met in Washington by their congressmen, and they went directly to a meeting at the Justice Department. Robert Kennedy stopped by and talked to them. The parents pleaded with Kennedy to not only help find their sons, but also to provide protection for all the other civil rights workers in Mississippi. Next the parents went to the White House. As they waited outside the Oval Office, the president received a call from J. Edgar Hoover, director of the FBI. Hoover told President Johnson that the blue Ford station wagon had been found in a swamp. The parents entered the office and Andrew's mother overheard the mention of the car and wanted to shout, "Tell me quickly. Are they all right?"

President Johnson held her hand and told the parents that the car had been badly burned. The "three kids" were still missing. He said, "I'm sorry to give you this news."

*Robert Kennedy*

The parents remained stoic and according to *Washington Post* columnist Drew Pearson, who was at the meeting, said "that they were proud of their sons and that, if it had to be done over again, they would still authorize the trip to Mississippi." The president assured them that the Justice and Defense departments would do everything in their power to find the missing young men.

Reporters at the Cincinnati airport told Rita and Mrs. Hamer, who was also there, that the burned car had been found. Mrs. Hamer drew Rita into her arms and they both cried. Rita said, "I knew then that they were dead."

*J. Edgar Hoover*

# CHAPTER SIX
# June 24, 1964

Photos of the charred station wagon jutting from the swamp appeared on the front pages of newspapers across the country. One headline read: WRECKAGE RAISES NEW FEARS OVER FATE OF MISSING MEN. Claude Sitton of the *New York Times* quoted an FBI source in Philadelphia who said, "Virtually all hope [has] faded . . . for the lives of three civil rights workers. . . . We're now looking for bodies."

Black leaders arrived in Neshoba County to help in the search. Dick Gregory, a black entertainer and civil rights activist, had been in the Soviet Union on an anti-nuclear-weapons ban-the-bomb mission when he heard of the disappearance. He quickly flew to Mississippi to lend his support and offered a reward of twenty-five thousand dollars to anyone finding the missing men and exposing those responsible for their disappearance. When Gregory and a caravan of sixteen cars carrying civil rights workers tried to drive into Neshoba County to investigate the ruins of Mount Zion Church and the area around the swamp, they were met at the Philadelphia city limits by Sheriff Rainey and 150 armed state police, and forced to turn back.

Meanwhile, in Philadelphia, FBI agents conspicuously dressed in dark suits, ties, and sunglasses, and carrying briefcases, went door to door questioning residents. No one would talk. Whites as well as blacks feared the Ku Klux Klan.

In Neshoba County locals fumed with anger over the national attention focused on the three missing civil rights workers, and voiced their comments.

"They had no business down here."

"COFO must have burned their own car to make the hoax look convincing."

"We don't think anything has happened to them, but if it has, they got what they deserved."

The Jackson *Clarion-Ledger* even claimed that Andrew Goodman had been seen boarding a bus in Baton Rouge, Louisiana.

Yet a few white citizens dared to speak out. A Philadelphia man said to the Rotary Club, "You know damn well our law is mixed up in this."

Ellen Spendrup, a native of Meridian, said that when the FBI men came to her house she would welcome them with Southern hospitality and offer them ice water. She and her niece Florence Mars cooperated with the FBI and provided background information about the community. As a result they were threatened and ostracized by their neighbors.

President Johnson called Senator James Eastland on his plantation in Ruleville, Mississippi, to ask what he thought of the situation.

Eastland said, "I don't believe there's three missing. I believe it's a publicity stunt." He denied there was any Ku Klux Klan activity and said, "Who could possibly harm them?"

Wednesday evening, Rita landed in Meridian. On the plane she had scribbled notes, and now she made a statement to the press. "I am going to find my husband and the other two people. I am going to find out what happened to them."

Rita said, "I suggest that if Mr. Chaney, a native Negro Mississippian, had been alone at the time of the disappearance, this case, like many before it, would have gone unnoticed." Reading from her notes, Rita delivered a list of demands. She wanted federal marshals to be sent into Mississippi for protection and an FBI investigation of reports that law enforcement officers had been involved in violent acts.

She told reporters she intended to go to Neshoba County and confront Sheriff Rainey in person. "I want to see what the sheriff has the nerve to say to me, if he has the nerve to repeat to me that it's a publicity stunt."

Rita believed that her husband and James knew the area too well to have done anything "foolhardy" when they were arrested, and that they would never have risked being arrested for speeding.

In Oxford, Ohio, Freedom Summer classes continued. The mood on campus "was like a funeral parlor," recalled a volunteer. The night before, at dinner, Moses had told the students that the station wagon had been found outside Philadelphia. "It's badly burned," he said quietly. "There is no news of the three boys."

Frantic parents called their children begging them to come home. An Oklahoma boy was forced to drop out when he received a letter from his father saying, "If you think you're going to liberate Mississippi, I'm getting a posse to liberate *you*."

Linda Davis's family appointed her father to go to Oxford and talk her out of going to Mississippi. "My dad pleaded with me to come back home," said Linda, age nineteen and an Oberlin student. She told him she couldn't do that, and he didn't insist. But he asked her to send him a postcard every day so that he would know if she was okay.

Psychiatrist Robert Coles talked with the students and sent eight frightened volunteers home. But he saw renewed spirit in the rest of the kids. "Suddenly hundreds of young Americans became charged with new energy and determination," he wrote.

The campus swarmed with reporters and TV cameramen. Photographers climbed over walls to snap pictures. "They followed us into the classrooms and dormitories, around the lounges, out along the paths," remembered Sally Belfrage. "There was footage, yardage, mileage of every face in the place."

Another girl said she kept seeing a movie camera aimed at her. "I wondered how I should look for my mother and father after I disappear," she said. "Smile, or look noble or what, you know, it seems to me that the most finally horrible thing in the world is posing for your own obituary photograph."

The next day, Thursday, June 25, the reporters' interviews with students were included in a CBS news special, "The Search in Mississippi." The kids crowded around the one television set on campus to watch. As they saw themselves singing "We Shall Overcome," they stood, arms crossed, holding hands SNCC style, and sang along with the television, "We shall overcome someday."

In Jackson, at the state capitol, Rita and two white civil rights veterans, Bob Zellner and Rev. Ed King, went to meet with the governor. Zellner, a

*George Wallace*

graduate student at Brandeis University, and King, a native Mississippian and Methodist minister, were turned away and told that Governor Paul Johnson was not in, so they walked over to the governor's elegant mansion with Rita. In the driveway Governor Johnson was getting out of his car with Governor George Wallace of Alabama, and was talking to reporters. Rita stood unnoticed.

A reporter asked Governor Johnson if there had been any developments in the case of the missing civil rights workers. "Governor Wallace and I are the only two people who know where they are," he joked, "and we're not telling."

Just then Wallace recognized Zellner, and he bolted into the mansion. Johnson lingered, talking to a reporter. Zellner stepped forward to shake his hand, and introduced Rita. The governor tried to pull away, but Zellner wouldn't release his grip.

A reporter shouted, "That's the wife of one of those missing men!"

A state trooper hurried over and yanked Zellner away. More state troopers surrounded Rita, Zellner, and King, and escorted them off the grounds.

The three went to the nearby federal building to meet with President Johnson's personal envoy, Allen Dulles. They repeated Governor Johnson's remark that he knew where the missing men were. Dulles insisted that they must have misunderstood. Rita grew angry. Dulles ended the interview and said, "I want to offer you my deepest sympathy."

"I don't want sympathy," Rita said. "I want my husband back."

# CHAPTER SEVEN
# June 25, 1964

On Thursday afternoon President Johnson ordered two hundred sailors from Meridian Naval Air Station to join the search for the three missing men.

"I imagine they're in that lake," he told an aide, referring to the swamp where the station wagon had been found. "It's my guess. Three days now."

The men wore white sailor hats and taped their pant legs to their ankles to keep the leeches out as they slogged through Bogue Chitto Swamp. They snapped branches from trees to use to fight off poisonous snakes. But they found nothing except Mickey's watch, which had stopped at 12:45.

The search was relocated to the area along Highway 19 where the three young men had last been seen. Then the sailors dragged the Pearl River, which runs through Neshoba County. Local whites watched and taunted them.

Meanwhile, in New York, Andrew's and Mickey's parents held a news conference in the Goodmans' apartment. Andrew's mother appealed to parents in Missisippi to cooperate in the search for the three young men, and ended her statement by giving the phone number of the FBI office in Meridian. She and Mickey's mother still held onto a hope that the boys might be in some jail or barn, somewhere.

In Meridian, Mrs. Chaney said little. Before James had left for Ohio, she had started making a quilt from scraps of her children's hand-me-down clothes. "It usually took Mama four days and plenty of scraps to make a queen-sized quilt," said Ben. "But this quilt has been in the frame since J. E. [James] came up missing. When Mama gonna finish this quilt?" he mumbled.

On Thursday night, Rita and Zellner returned to Meridian. She was more determined than ever to confront Rainey. Having heard that the sheriff had turned away Dick Gregory and the activists as they tried to enter Neshoba County, she and Zellner decided to slip in during the night.

In the early hours of Friday, June 26, while it was still dark, they left for Longdale. A white lawyer who had joined Freedom Summer went with them. Zellner drove a Corvair provided by CORE. Although it was equipped with a two-way radio for emergencies, he was panicked. For him, it was a "suicide mission." Rita, however, seemed fearless.

Before dawn they approached the burned-out Mount Zion Church. Cars and pickups were parked under the trees, guarding the site. The white vigilantes spotted the Corvair. A pickup truck raced toward them. Zellner floored it. The pickup chased the Corvair through the woods to Highway 16. Terrified, Zellner realized that they had almost become the victims of a second "disappearance."

The three then drove to the Delphia Courts Motel in Philadelphia, temporary headquarters of the FBI. Local "deputies" in pickups surrounded the motel.

In the parking lot Rita was introduced to an FBI agent.

"What are you trying to accomplish?" he said angrily. "You're going to get us all shot!"

Zellner started to explain that they wanted to see the burned station wagon and talk to Rainey. Just then the sheriff pulled into the motel parking lot accompanied by a Highway Patrol investigator, Charles Snodgrass, and a posse of men.

Rainey walked over to Rita and Zellner and said, "What in the goddamn hell are you doin' here?"

Rita said she wanted to see her husband's car.

Rainey shook his head and ordered her to leave the county immediately.

"I'm not leaving until I see Mickey's car," said Rita, "and I don't care how many pickup trucks show up to intimidate me."

Rainey agreed to talk to Rita, Zellner, and the lawyer in Rainey's patrol car. He and Snodgrass sat in the front seat. Rita said that she thought Rainey knew where her husband was. Snodgrass explained that Rainey had been visiting his wife in the hospital when Mickey was arrested, and therefore knew nothing.

Rita said to Rainey, "I'm not leaving here until I learn what happened to my husband. I'm going to keep drawing attention here until I find out, and if you don't like it you'll just have to have me killed, too."

Rainey said he'd give her five minutes with the car, then escort her to the city limits. Leading the way, he drove to Stokes Auto Body Shop. Rita, Zellner, and the lawyer followed in the Corvair and were tailed by a caravan of pickups. In the body shop, young white mechanics hooted and gave Rebel yells as Rita and Zellner viewed the blackened shell of the station wagon. It was mounted on blocks, it had no tires, and the windows were smashed. Rita had at last seen proof that she would never see Mickey again.

On Friday, June 27, in Oxford, Ohio, the students completed their orientation. They were "packed, scared, cheerful, and ready," said Sally Belfrage, who had chosen to be a librarian in Greenwood, Mississippi. That evening they all gathered in the auditorium.

A black staff member of SNCC led them in singing "We'll Never Turn Back." Then he said, "All of you should have nervousitis. If you have any doubts, we'll admire you for dropping out. But I think the best thing to say is, you know, we'll be there with you and . . . we'll never turn back."

Then Bob Moses took the microphone. His voice was low. He rubbed his eyes underneath his glasses and said softly, "The kids are dead."

He paused.

This was the first time those words had been spoken. Up to now the students had believed that the three young men had "simply 'disappeared.' "

"When we heard the news at the beginning," Moses went on, "I knew they were dead. When we heard they had been arrested I knew there had been a frame-up. We didn't say this earlier because of Rita, because she was really holding out for every hope. There may be more deaths. . . . I justify myself," said Moses, "because I'm taking risks myself, and I'm not asking people to do things I'm not willing to do. And the other thing is, people were being killed already, the Negroes of Mississippi."

The students listened with rapt attention, some crying. They sat where Andrew Goodman had sat the week before.

Moses said, "In our country we have some real evil, and the attempt to do something about it involves enormous effort. . . . If for any reason you're hesitant about what you're getting into, it's better for you to leave. Because what has got to be done has to be done in a certain way, or otherwise it won't get done."

"Moses, usually very steady, was breaking down as he said his last words to us," recalled Linda Davis.

He finished, stood for a moment, and slowly walked out of the auditorium. No one spoke. No one moved. Finally from the back of the room a woman named Jean Wheeler sang,

*They say freedom is a constant struggle.*
*They say freedom is a constant struggle.*

It was a new song, yet somehow everyone knew it and joined in.

*Oh, Lord, we've struggled so long,*
*We must be free, we must be free.*

# CHAPTER EIGHT

# End of June 1964

On Sunday, June 28, the new group of Freedom Summer workers rolled into Mississippi. This second group had prepared to create Freedom Schools. Now there were 450 volunteers scattered throughout the state, and white locals resented the "invasion."

"We're in the Memphis bus station right now, waiting for the bus to Ruleville," wrote Linda Davis on her first postcard home. "When we arrived this morning the police were here—5 emergency squad cars."

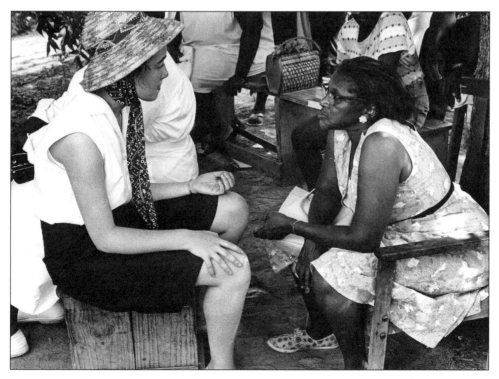

*Linda Davis, newly arrived in Ruleville, meeting her hostess, Mrs. Thomas*

*Porch of community center in Ruleville. Mrs. Hamer's SNCC campaign posters are on the wall.*

"Most of us would not have been too surprised if everybody had been arrested as we crossed the Miss. Border," wrote a volunteer in Ruleville.

"Violence hangs overhead like dead air," wrote another.

A student arriving at the train station in Jackson was kicked over from behind and slugged.

"I felt as strange as though I had gone to Mexico, except we spoke somewhat of a common language," recalled Fred Bright Winn. "It [the training program in Oxford] did not prepare me for the hate that people gave me, that white people gave me on the street; the glares, the words, the finger, the absolute hate that you felt walking down the street."

Len Edwards said, "The first night I was there [in Ruleville], I was eating a hamburger and two guys came to me and said, 'We think you should go home now. There are a lot of crazies around here. We're telling you for your own safety.'"

Twenty students got off the Greyhound bus in Ruleville and were stared down by white men drinking beer. The sheriff drove up in a truck with a menacing German shepherd in back. Just at that moment Mrs. Hamer came along and took all of the volunteers to her house for lunch. They sat outside on benches in the shade of a huge pecan tree. Linda Davis had chosen to go to Sunflower County because of Mrs. Hamer. She had been frightened about going since the announcement of the disappearance of the three civil rights workers on the first day of orientation. But then Linda met Mrs. Hamer at Oxford and heard her speak. "Watching her unflinching courage, her commitment to 'keep on keeping on, no matter what,' just made me fall in love with her," said Davis. "She was such a mesmerizing force that I determined to follow her to Ruleville."

The civil rights workers had set up headquarters in Mrs. Hamer's parlor. The newcomers met Len Edwards and the volunteers who had arrived the previous Sunday. The volunteers said that as they were canvassing, white men had thrown stones and trash at them and yelled insults. In the town of

Itta Bena three civil rights workers were forcibly taken to the bus stop and ordered to leave town immediately or "never leave." They stayed.

In Greenwood, Sally Belfrage said, "the week had been hard, not just from the tension of the three boys' disappearance, but because of harassment."

Len Edwards had a car and drove Mrs. Hamer to neighboring towns "to stir people up to register to vote," and said, "My car was firebombed and trashed."

Police joined in the harassment. They arrested volunteers for any excuse: speeding, reckless driving, and even "reckless walking." A car swerved at a white woman and a black woman walking together in Greenwood. They jumped out of the way, and as the car passed they noticed a sticker in the rear window: YOU ARE IN OCCUPIED MISSISSIPPI: PROCEED WITH CAUTION.

COFO kept a running list of daily "incidents" that included threats, arrests, bombings, beatings, and shootings. Stokely Carmichael, project director in the Mississippi Delta, told new recruits that he had just been in Philadelphia. "All the whites are out on the corners with their guns," he said. "I'll bet seventy percent of them know what happened to the boys."

Len Edwards, a law student from the University of Chicago, was the only lawyer in the Summer Project, and said, "The FBI followed me everywhere. J. Edgar Hoover, director of the FBI, supported the white Southerners." Edwards had arrived before Freedom Summer began, and was staying in Ruleville in a "ramshackle house" riddled with bullet holes, next door to Mrs. Hamer's. Before he drove to Mississippi Mrs. Hamer had sent him a handwritten letter. "The Highway Patrol will be waiting for you at the border," she warned. "There have been some shootings down here. I'm glad you're coming down but be careful."

Black Mississippians welcomed the students. Mrs. Bernice White in Indianola said, "We were glad to see them . . . because here no white educated people talked to us, and here were young people from big cities and places, and we found out that they were just like anyone else. They were friendly, and we were happy to have them around. We found out that they would eat the same thing that we would eat,

*Len Edwards canvassing in the Delta*

*SNCC photographer running away from the sheriff*

because whatever we were eating, if they came in, they ate right along with us."

A volunteer in Meridian wrote about the old men and women who stopped him as he was leaving church after addressing the congregation. "[They] press a dollar into your hand and say, 'I've waited 80 years for you to come and I just have to give you this little bit to let you all know how much we appreciate your coming.' "

*Voter registration canvassing. Hattiesburg resident Horace Laurence (left) and Freedom Summer volunteer Dick Landerman (right) sitting on Laurence's front porch*

Geoff, a volunteer in Batesville, described how he and his group were warmly received by the black community: "Children and adults waved from their porches and shouted hello as we walked along," he wrote. "In a few days scores of children knew us and called us by name. We had been warned to expect fear and hostility, but we were immediately invited to live and eat in Negro houses and to speak in Negro churches. For many local citizens our coming was a religious event."

Andy Schiffrin was living with the Waterhouse family in Meridian, in "the poor part of town." Their house was "simple but well kept up," he said. "Their three daughters were so energetic."

*Children in Ruleville*

"The girls are always asking questions," he wrote to his parents. Andy became close to the girls and Rosalyn, age eleven, wrote a letter to his mother Shirley in San Diego. "Andy is a real nice boy, he's a part of the family to us. . . . We took some pictures sunday [sic], and he went to church with us. Everyone was real nice to him at church. They asked him to come back again."

Tracy Sugarman, the older artist and writer, had followed McLaurin to Ruleville and was assigned to stay with the Williams family. When Sugarman was introduced to Mr. Williams they

*Rosalyn Waterhouse*

shook hands. "It's very generous of you and Mrs. Williams to open your house to us this way," said Sugarman. There were tears in Mr. Williams's eyes and he couldn't speak. Later he said to Sugarman, "I'm sorry I couldn't welcome you befo'. . . . I was jus' so filled up, meetin' you . . . in my house I couldn't talk. . . . It's a fine, Christian thing, a fine thing that you all have come here."

Mr. and Mrs. Oscar Giles, owners of the Penny Saver grocery in Indianola, hosted volunteers in their house adjoining the store. "Mama told us there were going to be people staying at our house," recalled their son Dr. Eugene Giles, who was nine years old at the time. "I had to give up my bed the way I did when my uncle and aunt drove from Arizona and arrived at 2 or 3 a.m. It was the first time people of another color persuasion were staying with us. It was kind of different. Maybe there are some nice white people," he thought.

Black families risked their lives in hosting "outsiders." Many were prepared for trouble. Mr. Giles, who was active in the civil rights movement, made thick wire screens to cover the windows of the grocery store and the front room of the house. If someone threw a firebomb it would bounce off the screen. "Before we'd go to bed," remembered Dr. Giles, "he'd say, 'Time to put the screens on the windows.'" One night he didn't do it, and that night, May 1, 1965, the house was firebombed and almost totally destroyed. On the same night Mrs. Magruder's house was burned to the ground.

But at the beginning of Freedom Summer in 1964, "Mrs. Magruder said she 'was not afraid.' She would do 'whatever she could to help the movement,'" wrote John Harris, an African-American volunteer who had a room in her house.

Mrs. Magruder's great-nieces, Stacy and Marsha White, five-year-old twins,

*Mr. and Mrs. Williams with their grandchild*

lived in Indianola and came over with their mother, Bernice White, to visit. "And the Freedom Summer volunteers would visit us at our home on Roosevelt Street," recalled Stacy. The little girls played with the volunteers. "I knew these people as playmates," said Stacy. "They were very kind. They were different from white Southerners. They treated us with respect and dignity." Once, when Stacy was at her great-aunt's house, the volunteers gave her a "fluffy white cat" and she took it home. But later "on the very same day the cat ran off." Stacy, who thought the volunteers would think she didn't like her gift started to cry. Her mother said, "Why are you crying?" And Stacy said, "They think I don't want the cat."

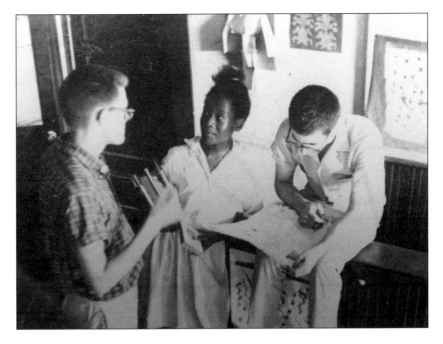

*Left to right: Joe Morse, Rosalyn Waterhouse, and Ronald deSouza*

Stacy and Marsha's two older sisters would bring books home that had been donated for the Freedom Schools. Their mother helped sort the truckloads of books, clothes, and supplies that arrived at Mrs. Magruder's.

Dr. Giles recalled that his family's house and grocery store were nearby and served as a holding place till the donations could be distributed at church. "Mom would catalogue the things," he said. Sometimes the donations included toys. Once he was helping sort the stuff and found a camera, "a gray box type."

"Please let me have it," he said to his mom. She did. It was his first camera. "It was a big deal," said Dr. Giles, "and I kept that for years."

Jo, a volunteer in Canton, wrote, "Our hostesses are brave women. . . . The other morning a local newscaster said that someone was reported to have offered someone else $400 to bomb all the houses where volunteers

*Marsha and Stacy White*

*A pile for "Language," a pile for "History," a pile for "crud"*

are staying." Jo's hostess slept with a hatchet under her pillow to protect herself.

Another volunteer wrote, "One family got scared and asked two of us to leave after a car parked all night in front of their home a couple of nights ago. . . . Another person was fired from his job yesterday because two of us were staying with him."

But "the Negroes were beginning to see the students as people they knew and trusted," observed Sugarman. "The students' camaraderie with the Negroes was as easy as it was inevitable. Cut off from the white world they knew, they were finding comfort and warmth within the Negro community."

"Reentering the Negro quarter feels more like seeking sanctuary every day," he wrote in his journal after driving a carload of people to Drew to help them register to vote. "Crossing a main highway is hazardous, a trip to town is a watchful enterprise, and often you find a car tailing you. You return to the quarter and you breathe easier."

*Seal's Grocery on Highway 41. "Downtown in black Ruleville"*

# CHAPTER NINE
# June 29, 1964

There was still no trace of Mickey, James, and Andy. Posters with their mug shots appeared throughout the South with the words MISSING—CALL FBI.

On Monday, June 29, Rita flew to Washington with Bob Zellner to meet with President Johnson. It had been a week since the three men had disappeared, and Rita felt that not enough was being done to find them.

President Johnson was more than a foot taller than she was and more than twice her weight, but Rita was not intimidated. "We've come to talk about three missing people in Mississippi," she said. "We've come to talk about a search that we don't think is being done seriously."

"I'm sorry you feel that way, Miss," said the president.

Rita demanded that five thousand federal marshals be sent to Mississippi immediately. The president replied that he couldn't send "thousands of men," but everything that could be done was being done. Later Rita said to reporters, "When the federal authorities pull out of Philadelphia, Mississippi, I tremble at what is going to happen to the Negroes in the area."

The FBI continued its investigation and questioned nearly two thousand people. Half of those interviewed were thought to be members of the Klan. The rest were relatives or neighbors of Klansmen, and nearly all of them refused to cooperate. "In spirit, everyone belonged to the Klan," said Inspector Joseph Sullivan, who headed the team. Rewards as high as fifty thousand dollars were offered in the hopes that someone would come forward with information. No one claimed the reward. FBI agents stuffed candy into their pockets and gave it to kids who talked about their parents' activities. But even black citizens mistrusted the federal agents. They feared the agents would report back to the local police.

Frogmen assisted the FBI in dragging the muddy waters of the Old

# MISSING CALL FBI

THE FBI IS SEEKING INFORMATION CONCERNING THE DISAPPEARANCE AT PHILADELPHIA, MISSISSIPPI, OF THESE THREE INDIVIDUALS ON JUNE 21, 1964. EXTENSIVE INVESTIGATION IS BEING CONDUCTED TO LOCATE GOODMAN, CHANEY, AND SCHWERNER, WHO ARE DESCRIBED AS FOLLOWS:

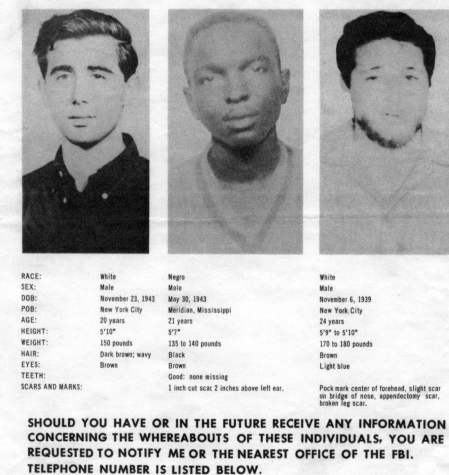

| | ANDREW GOODMAN | JAMES EARL CHANEY | MICHAEL HENRY SCHWERNER |
|---|---|---|---|
| RACE: | White | Negro | White |
| SEX: | Male | Male | Male |
| DOB: | November 23, 1943 | May 30, 1943 | November 6, 1939 |
| POB: | New York City | Meridian, Mississippi | New York City |
| AGE: | 20 years | 21 years | 24 years |
| HEIGHT: | 5'10" | 5'7" | 5'9" to 5'10" |
| WEIGHT: | 150 pounds | 135 to 140 pounds | 170 to 180 pounds |
| HAIR: | Dark brown; wavy | Black | Brown |
| EYES: | Brown | Brown | Light blue |
| TEETH: | | Good: none missing | |
| SCARS AND MARKS: | | 1 inch cut scar 2 inches above left ear. | Pock mark center of forehead, slight scar on bridge of nose, appendectomy scar, broken leg scar. |

**SHOULD YOU HAVE OR IN THE FUTURE RECEIVE ANY INFORMATION CONCERNING THE WHEREABOUTS OF THESE INDIVIDUALS, YOU ARE REQUESTED TO NOTIFY ME OR THE NEAREST OFFICE OF THE FBI. TELEPHONE NUMBER IS LISTED BELOW.**

June 29, 1964

DIRECTOR
FEDERAL BUREAU OF INVESTIGATION
UNITED STATES DEPARTMENT OF JUSTICE
WASHINGTON, D. C. 20535
TELEPHONE, NATIONAL 8-7117

FBI/DOJ

River bayou. To their horror they found the remains of several black corpses: routine victims of Klan murders. Among the bodies identified were Henry H. Dee and his friend Charlie Eddie Moore, both nineteen. It was learned that the Klan murdered Dee because he came from Chicago and was thought to be the ringleader of a Black Muslim plot. They killed Moore for participating in a protest demonstration at his college, Alcorn A&M, in Lorman, Mississippi. Later another corpse, fished from the Big Black River. It was the body of a fourteen-year-old boy wearing a CORE T-shirt. He was identified as Herbert Oarsby.

"But we have to keep dragging rivers and beating the bushes while the *real* search goes on," said a federal agent, "the search for that citizen who, for protection and money, will eventually take us to the bodies."

While the families of the missing men spent agonizing days waiting for news, they were tormented by crank calls and expressions of hatred. One person demanded a ransom from Andrew Goodman's mother to get her son back. "You know, five thousand dollars isn't much for your boy's life," said the caller.

"Could it be true?" wondered Carolyn Goodman. "Could there be some terrorists holding on to the kids and just wanting money?"

In Meridian people phoned Mrs. Chaney and threatened to bomb her house. "Crosses burned on the lawn," said Ben. "The house was shot in a couple of times. They fired her from her job." When Mrs. Chaney went to the state employment office and tried to get another job as a maid, the counselor said to her, "Who would want you now after the way you've scandalized Mississippi whites?"

Despite the mounting tension, student volunteers "stifled their fears" and went to work. They got used to the gnats, the heat, and the dampness. Fred Bright Winn, a twenty-year-old volunteer from San Francisco, was the only volunteer who had brought tools: hammer, nails, saw, measuring tape, wrenches. "I had been working with my uncle who started me in the plumbing trade," he said. "The building [in Ruleville] that was to become the Freedom School was an old two-level house. The school needed library shelves, doors hung, a toilet repaired, and security panels for the windows at nighttime. . . . Of course we had very little money. In the yard there was an outhouse that had since been closed. It was a leftover from the time when there wasn't a sewer system on the 'colored' side of town. . . . To me it was just a structure made of great book shelving. We tore it down, removed the nails, and made a Freedom Library with it." Laughing kids helped to build bookshelves with the smelly planks. By the end of the day they had created the Ruleville Freedom School.

Winn and his team had no assigned place to stay at first, so they bunked in the Freedom School they were working on. "Now that was scary," he said.

*Indianola Freedom School firebombed. The building had been a center for voter registration meetings and a Freedom School.*

"Freedom Schools were the first targets in each town to be firebombed. Each night we would hang plywood over the windows so a bomb could not come crashing through. I used as few nails as possible in the plywood over the window where I slept so if need be I could kick it out and escape. But it was so, so hot inside. Keeping the bare light bulb in the room burning made it that much hotter. We lay on the matrices [sic] listening to each car, each dog barking, every sound, fearing that the next would be a Molotov cocktail crashing against the building."

Winn could not get used to the "threat of death." In a letter to his dad he wrote about the disappearance of Mickey, Andy, and James. "Dad, I hope you realize that I may be in that same position in a few days."

Local people who dared to house volunteers and come to the community centers and Freedom Schools had been courageously confronting danger for years in their struggle for civil rights.

"Many faced real scary stuff," said Rita Schwerner.

"There was violence," recalled Mrs. Bernice White, the niece of Mrs. Irene Magruder. "When she [Mrs. Magruder] opened up her house and some of them would need protection sometimes, that's when they would go to my father and see could they get a gun . . . because the civil rights people didn't have guns. . . . I made a register for those who come to my aunt's house. They were coming from so many different places that I knew I couldn't remember them all. . . . Fannie Lou Hamer brought several people there with her sometimes when she came."

*Mrs. Hamer at a citizenship class*

Later that summer when Mrs. Hamer told her story on national television, she said, *"Is this America?* The land of the free and the home of the brave? Where we have to sleep with our telephones off of the hooks because our lives be threatened daily?"

"They were all at risk," said Andy Schiffrin, a guest of the Waterhouse family. "The older group was more cynical, less optimistic about the possibility of change. Mothers were critical of letting their kids participate. But the kids were sure change was going to come. Their rights were worth fighting for."

# CHAPTER TEN
# Early July 1964

Inspector Sullivan ordered his FBI agents to keep seeking information about the three missing men. The case had to be solved. Agents chased down each lead. Search parties scoured every acre and dirt road in Neshoba County.

*Neshoba County Sheriff Lawrence Rainey (left) and his deputy, Cecil Price*

"The pressure from Washington for some solution—at least as to the whereabouts of the victims—was really intense," said Sullivan. His team grew weary and discouraged, but Sullivan remained optimistic. "He perceived the historical importance of the case," said an agent. "So long as people were dying on lonely back roads in the South, in Mississippi, being lynched by vigilante groups that most likely included Baptist preachers and even the police, no one was safe."

The FBI was growing suspicious of Sheriff Rainey. Rainey, a big man with an eighth-grade education, wore Western garb and carried a pair of six-shooters. Everyone knew he had killed two unarmed black men while he was on duty. Once, when Rainey was a policeman in Philadelphia, he had ordered Luther Jackson, a black man seated in a parked car with his former girlfriend, to get out. Jackson, a Philadelphia native, had moved to Chicago and was visiting. As he attempted to get out of the car Rainey shot him to death. Rainey claimed that Jackson had thrown him to the ground and was choking him. A black woman, Frances Culbertson, happened to witness the scene. When Sheriff Hop Barnett arrived she said, "How could you let him [Rainey] kill a good man like this?" Weeks later Culbertson was arrested and roughed up in jail by Rainey. No other witnesses came forward, and Rainey was cleared of wrongdoing.

Another time when Rainey was a deputy sheriff he had responded to a call at a black home where a twenty-seven-year-old epileptic had gone on a rampage. Rainey and Barnett handcuffed the young man and started driving him to the mental hospital. On the way either Barnett or Rainey shot the man. Later they claimed that he had tried to grab a gun from the glove compartment although he was in handcuffs. The coroner declared the shooting "justifiable homicide."

Rainey's excessive brutality was legendary. He and his deputy, Cecil Price, had a reputation for terrorizing blacks. A patrolman in Meridian finally gave the FBI a list of seven names of people who might have taken part in the crime against the three civil rights workers. "I have no proof," said the patrolman, "but I bet you every one of these men was involved in this." Among the names were Sheriff Rainey and Deputy Price.

On July 2 the FBI called in Rainey for questioning at their headquarters in the Delphia Courts Motel. They showed him pictures of Mickey, James, and Andrew. "Never seen them before," the sheriff lied. He said that on the night of June 21 he had visited his wife in the hospital, then had dinner with relatives, and returned to Philadelphia before midnight.

Price was also brought in. Both he and Rainey insisted on having a lawyer present, confirming the FBI's suspicions. Sullivan was sure that they knew more than they were telling.

That evening at 7 p.m., President Johnson signed the Civil Rights Act outlawing segregation in all public facilities. Network programming was interrupted and the ceremony was televised nationally. Standing behind the president and looking on were several congressmen and Dr. Martin Luther King Jr. President Johnson entreated Americans to "close the springs of racial poison."

*President Johnson signs the Civil Rights Act.*

Over the weekend, members of the NAACP tested the law in Southern restaurants, movie theaters, and hotels. Some places accepted black customers for the first time.

But many white Mississippians refused to comply with the new law, swearing, "Never!" In Philadelphia a hostile crowd watched the NAACP delegation enter the

*Freedom School class at Mt. Zion Baptist Church, Hattiesburg*

Neshoba County Courthouse. The WHITES ONLY and COLORED signs above the drinking fountains and bathrooms had not been removed. When the group asked permission to see the ruins of Mount Zion Methodist Church and the area where the burned station wagon had been found, they were refused. When Deputy Price shouted, "Get out of town! Get going!" the group fled for their lives.

*Freedom School registration sign*

SNCC leaders told Freedom Summer workers to not test the newly passed Civil Rights Act and to stay out of confrontations. A volunteer wrote home, "People here in Clarksdale know all about that bill, but tomorrow and Saturday, the 4th of July, they will still be in the cotton fields making three dollars a day. . . . They'll still be starving and afraid."

Nevertheless, the volunteers celebrated Independence Day. In Clarksdale, Aaron "Doc" Henry, a leading black spokesperson, invited volunteers to his place for hot dogs.

In Ruleville, Mrs. Hamer threw a picnic, and volunteers ate

8:30 - Freedom and the Negro in America  In this course we will study
problems of the Negro in Mississippi, the Negro in the North,
Myths about the Negro, Who runs things in the South, Common
problems of Negroes and Whites, the Freedom Movement, and
Negro history.  Through reading, listening, and just talking
about our thoughts, we hope to understand better what a
society is and swhat our soc_ty society is.  Understanding
this, we will be able to think better about just why we want
freedom and what we mean when we say we want freedom.

10:00 - English  In this course we promise never to talk about things
like "adjectives," "participles," and "semicolons."  We are
interested in helping you say what you are thinking and learn
to writeddown what you are thinking and write so that other
people can understand what you are trying to say;  we are interested in helping you to read and to criticize and understand what you read.  Some of our reading will be Negro literature.

11:00 - Electives  We will have two periods of electives, one at 11
and one at 1.  If you want to study one subject thoroughly,
(such as American History and Government or a foreign language) sign for the same course at both hours.  Otherwise,
you cam select two different subjects.

        American History and Government
        Negro History
        Current Events
        Literature
        Foreign Languages
        Math - all levels
        Science - any kind, any level (we think)
        Art

12:00  Lunch

1:00   Electives

2:00   Clubs  Clubs will meet two or three times a week.  You may
       sign for one or two.

        Newspaper              Music
        Art                    Sports
        Typing                 Public Speaking
        Tutorials (indivi-     Drama
        dual help in aca-      Mississippi Student Union
        demic subjects)        Canvassing and Political Action

------------------------------------------------------------------------

EVENING CLASSES FOR ADULTS

7:30   Freedom and the Negro in America (see description above)
       We will learn mostly by talking and sharing experiences.

8:30   Electives (see above)  Also Reading.

------------------------------------------------------------------------

*COFO Freedom Summer registration form with schedule*

special dishes prepared by local women. The menu included corn bread,
peas in bacon and onion sauce, potato casseroles, and pies and cakes and
ice cream. After the feast a black woman spoke: "These young folk who
are already free, they come here only to help us. They is proving to us that
black and white can do it together."

From Ruleville, Linda Davis wrote a card to her family:

"We open school tomorrow—We're not really sure of how many people will come but many have come to help as we've cleaned the place up. In the morning—women + their young children. In the afternoon—students, and in the evening any more adults who wish to come. I will be teaching literacy among other things. Everything is still fine—we're all hoping."

During the first days of July, Freedom Schools opened across the state and volunteers canvassed door-to-door, trying to register voters. In Meridian, where Mickey and Rita had started their work, fifty students were expected at the new Freedom School, and 120 showed up. Children ran in and out, adults studied citizenship, and some started learning how to read. Volunteers were thrilled with the turnout.

*Ann in Ruleville. She was five or six and had to take care of her younger siblings.*

"I tutored an adult man in reading," recalled Vicki Halper, a volunteer from Oberlin who was in Greenville.

On Tuesday Linda Davis sent a card to her parents that began with illegible marks made by one of her students. "This says Ann," wrote Linda, explaining the scrawl. "She's 5 years old + was watching me write. There are 4 other kids younger than her whom she's supposed to take care of. Kids grow up fast here."

*Ann (the tallest) with her four siblings. Linda Davis learned they all perished in a fire caused by a space heater.*

Andy Schiffrin reported from Meridian that his host's three daughters, Lelia Jean, Rosalyn, and Patricia, had "incredible energy" and were going to the Freedom School and community center all the time.

Gail, another volunteer in Meridian, described the school in a letter to her parents: "The Freedom School is an old Baptist Seminary,

*Volunteers cleaning up the community center in Hattiesburg*

which was supposed to be condemned last year. We are thankful for it. We are one of the few Freedom Schools with a building of our own and classrooms and desks and blackboards. I teach two sections of a course called Freedom and the Negro in America—we talk about things like 'What do we mean when we say, "Things are Bad in Mississippi"?' 'What do white people have that we want?' 'What do they have that we don't want?' And I am teaching French to the younger kids, mostly 11 to 14. I never expected to come to Mississippi to teach French but they love it."

Elinor Tideman was also teaching at the Meridian Freedom School. "The women from the church every day would bring food for all the teachers," she recalled. "I used to look forward to it so much. . . . They had fried chicken and deviled eggs and potato salad. . . . They would spread it out on the table. . . . It was so touching to be cared for that way. . . . I felt like I belonged; I felt like they liked me and wanted me to be there."

A volunteer teaching at a Freedom School in Hattiesburg wrote, "My students are from 13 to 17 years old, and not one of them has heard

*Freedom School class on the church lawn*

about the Supreme Court decision of 1954 [banning segregation in public schools]. I don't need to tell them that segregation is wrong, and that separate-but-equal is a myth; but they are surprised to hear that the law is on their side, because they hear only about the laws of Mississippi in their school."

Tracy Sugarman, the older reportorial artist, observed the first day of classes at the Ruleville Freedom School. At 8:15 in the morning Linda Davis was teaching older women to read. Meanwhile, in the next room, four- through seven-year-olds explored the bookshelves. "Heidi Dole [a volunteer teacher], her pretty face animated with pleasure, was handing books to the bright-eyed youngsters," wrote Sugarman. "They would curl up on the floor and excitedly thumb through the volumes in search of pictures and color. A world beyond the Delta began to unfold, and a wonderful silence fell on the room."

Afternoon sessions were held for the older children. "In groups of three and four, teachers led their students to areas of the lawn where they might discuss and question without interrupting the progress of another group," wrote Sugarman. "I watched the young teachers starting to probe, gently urging their wide-eyed kids to ask, to be curious, to dare to try."

At some Freedom Schools and community centers black teenage boys read copies of *Ebony*, a magazine published by and for African Americans, for the first time. *Ebony* featured articles ranging from profiles of singer Aretha Franklin and actor Sidney Poitier to tips on hair styling.

*Volunteer Arthur Reese (standing) talking to a group of teenage male Freedom School students who sit on or near the porch of a house on Gavel Line Street reading issues of* Ebony *magazine*

*Kathy Rubel, a volunteer from California, teaching children in Ruleville community center*

The schools and community centers were overenrolled and drew enthusiastic crowds. Mel Canal, a volunteer in Meridian, "was very popular with the kids," recalled his coworker Alan Reich. "Mel had been a varsity athlete at San Jose State, water polo and soccer," said Alan. "I can remember the fun the kids had with him, having a catch with Mel, returning the balls with his feet or head, never his hands, something they'd never seen." Students ran their own newspapers and performed original plays. Adults and teens took classes in sewing, typing, and nutrition. Linda Davis even taught a class in modern dance. "The kids were panting, trying to keep up," recalled Sugarman, who was sketching the girls "gambol across the sunbaked earth in Ruleville."

And the girls taught their teachers how to flap their arms and do "the Monkey."

However, voter registration was not going as well. In the town of Drew, Len Edwards went canvassing. Late one afternoon he went up to the porch of a broken-down house. The men were just in from the cotton fields and some of the women were wearing maids' uniforms. Len introduced himself and said, "We're on a voter registration drive and we'd like to have you join us." No one responded. Finally someone said, "I don't know about that." And the conversation ended. Len tried

*Two children in the Freedom Library, Palmer's Crossing community center*

other houses down the street. "Don't you want to register?" he said. Usually the answer was no. Occasionally he got a yes, but the talk went no further.

"There has not been much reaction from the people of Drew," Len wrote to his parents, "but this is quite understandable. There are several reasons including fear of the white community (including the police), and apathy for anything out of the ordinary. We are however, making progress; some of the fear has been overcome. . . . In a few days we hope to have a 'freedom day' (usually lasting for a couple of weeks) during which time we will try to register all of the negroes in the county. . . . This means we will have to overcome the Mississippi voter registration requirements which include interpreting a portion of the 1890 Mississippi constitution."

"It's going to be a rough summer," Len told James Atwater, a reporter who was covering the story for the *Saturday Evening Post* magazine. "It's going to be a matter of plugging along day by day."

*Len Edwards and his father, Congressman Don Edwards, speaking to Joe McDonald at his home in Ruleville*

# CHAPTER ELEVEN
# July and early August 1964

By now everyone assumed that Mickey, James, and Andrew were dead. The president was impatient for a breakthrough in the investigation. On July 10, J. Edgar Hoover arrived in Jackson and opened an FBI office in an abandoned bank. Hoover assured the president that he would discover what had happened to the men. Posters with pictures of the three appeared throughout America, in post offices, banks, police stations, and courthouses. Magazines featured the three faces.

"The ghosts of those three shadow all our work," wrote a volunteer. 'Did you know them?' I am constantly asked."

A reporter from a San Diego radio station asked Andy Schiffrin the same question over the phone: "Did you have contact with either of these three men before they disappeared?"

"Yes," said Andy. "There were eight of us who drove down from Oxford, Ohio, together. . . . We all knew that Mississippi had incidents of violence for many, many years. . . . We were told that some of us might be killed, most of us might be jailed or beaten or both. It was something that we had to live with and hope for the best."

An article in the *Los Angeles Times* quoted Andy as saying that he was " 'frightened' but determined to finish his 'commitment' in the South."

Hoover left Jackson without any new information. He told the president, "Solution, while certain, will take some time. . . . Instructions have been issued that no amount of material, manpower, or expense is to be spared."

In the middle of July, Inspector Sullivan received a fresh lead. Florence Mars, a white native of Meridian, told him that Wilmer Jones, a black teenager with a goatee like Mickey's, had been arrested by Sheriff Rainey that spring. Upon Wilmer's release from jail, he was turned over to a group of whites who drove him around the Neshoba countryside questioning him about his "civil rights activities" while holding a gun to his neck and threatening to kill him. They took him to a secluded location they called "the place." Sullivan believed that this was what had happened to Mickey, James, and Andrew.

Wilmer had survived the ordeal and had moved to Chicago, so FBI agents found him and took a statement. Wilmer agreed to return to Philadelphia to help the FBI find that "place." As agents drove him around, Wilmer wore a paper bag with eye slits over his head to protect his identity. He was forced to duck down when other cars passed. After two days of searching, Wilmer led the agents to a spot a few miles southwest of Philadelphia. The FBI concentrated their search on that part of Neshoba County.

Klansmen grew nervous. They feared Wilmer and worried that he was a civil rights worker trying to "take over" the state of Mississippi. It was obvious to them that the FBI was "getting warm." The bureau had offered a new and bigger reward for anyone willing to reveal where the bodies were hidden. Sullivan's boss issued a statement: "The FBI is interested in but one thing at this time and that [is] to find the victims. . . . We would then pay a substantial amount of money, indicated to be from five thousand to thirty thousand dollars."

Although the offer was tempting, any Klansman knew that if he came forward and spoke he would be asking to get himself shot or worse. No one talked.

But on July 31, a citizen of Neshoba known as "Mr. X" informed the FBI where the bodies were buried and arranged to receive the reward. The man's identity was withheld even from the Justice Department.

On Saturday, August 1, Inspector Sullivan acted on the tip and scouted the property known as Old Jolly Farm. The informant had described a large earthen dam, but the agents couldn't find it in the densely wooded area. Sullivan ordered a team to fly over the farm to try to spot the dam from the air. Guided by the pilots, the agents hiked through the piney woods to a clearing. They saw the dam, but the digging tools they had brought with them were inadequate.

On Tuesday, August 4, armed with a search warrant and heavy earthmoving equipment, the agents returned to the dam at 8:00 a.m. and sealed off the property, posting guards at the perimeter.

"Where are we going to start?" asked one of the agents. Jay

Cochran Jr., who was in charge of the excavation, picked up a stick, walked about thirty paces, and stabbed the earth. "We'll start here," he said.

Perhaps it was luck or maybe it was a tip from Mr. X. The stick marked the exact spot where the bodies were buried. As the excavation proceeded, Cochran assigned jobs to the other agents. One man kept a log. Another mapped the dam and the surrounding land. A third collected items of evidence, and someone else stood by with a camera.

It was a stifling hot day, 106 degrees, and the agents worked all morning in their shirtsleeves. Sullivan, who was at the Delphia Courts Motel, kept in touch with them by walkie-talkie. At 11 a.m. one of the agents noticed an unusual smell, "the faint odor of decaying organic material." Cochran slowed down the machinery, and agents began digging with garden tools. At 2:50 p.m. an agent jotted in his logbook, "The pungent odor of decaying flesh is clearly discernible."

Blowflies swarmed into the pit, buzzards circled overhead.

The heels of a man's boots poked out of the earth. The agents silently dug with shovels and their bare hands. Gently they scraped away. At 3:18 p.m. they saw the outline of a man's form encased in the red clay. Two hours later they unearthed the body of Mickey Schwerner. At 5:07 a second corpse was found. It was Andrew Goodman. At 5:14 James Chaney's body was uncovered.

An agent took photographs. Sullivan was notified. Word was sent to Washington. Sullivan brought Deputy Price to the site to observe his reaction. Price remained unemotional as the bodies were picked up, placed in plastic bags, and tagged. He helped carry the bags to the hearse that drove them to the University of Mississippi Medical Center in Jackson for autopsies. That night the families of the boys were notified. At 8:45 regular programming on radio and TV was interrupted, and a special bulletin came on with the breaking news.

In Meridian the famous American folk singer Pete Seeger was giving a concert. Volunteers in the audience sang along as Seeger strummed his banjo. Then someone came onstage and handed him a note. He lowered his eyes and told the news to the crowd. There were gasps and tears.

"We must sing 'We Shall Overcome' now," said Seeger. "The three boys would not have wanted us to weep now, but to sing and understand this song." Then he led the audience in singing "O Healing River" and one song after another to bring comfort and sustain hope.

When reporters asked Rita for comments, she said, "I think three very good men were killed, men who could have made unbelievable contributions to American life."

Mrs. Chaney said, "My boy died a martyr for something he believed in—I believe in—and as soon as his little brother Ben gets old enough he'll take James's place as a civil rights worker."

*Volunteers and local residents sing "We Shall Overcome" at Three Light Baptist Church in Hattiesburg*

# THE STUDENT VOICE

VOL. 5 NO. 21      STUDENT VOICE, INC.      6 Raymond Street, N. W.      Atlanta, Georgia 30314      AUGUST 19, 1964

THE THREE MOTHERS OF THE THREE SLAIN RIGHTS WORKERS leave service for Andrew Goodman. Mrs. Chaney, Mrs. Goodman and Mrs. Schwerner (l ro r) leave the Ethical Society auditorium after services for the slain worker.

# NATION MOURNS SLAIN WORKERS

PHILADELPHIA, MISS.-Neshoba County Sheriff Lawrence Rainey refused to speak to FBI agents investigating the death of three civil rights workers.

Approached by two agents, Rainey asked if they had a warrant. When they replied "no," Rainey told the agents, "Come and see me when you got one and I'll be glad to talk to you."

Meanwhile, services were held for the three slain workers.

Memorial services were held in Meridian, Miss. for James Chaney and in New York City for Andrew Goodman and Michael Schwerner.

Concurrent memorial services have been held throughout the country to commemorate the workers' deaths.

In Mississippi, the FBI was reported to be keeping several persons under surveillance while it searched for a weapon to match the bullets taken from the bodies.

Dr. David Spain, a New York physician, who examined the body of Chaney, reported that he found evidence of a severe beating, probably with a blunt instrument.

Pathologists in Jackson found five bullets, three in Chaney, one each in Goodman and Schwerner.

## OMNIBUS RIGHTS SUIT FILED AGAINST MISS.

JACKSON, MISS. - A suit asking that 16 laws which hinder civil rights activities be struck down has been filed by Mississippi rights leaders.

The suit, filed in U.S. District Court here, contends that the laws abridge freedom of speech, press, right to assemble peacefully, petition for redress of grievances and have deprived Negroes of "life, liberty, and property without due process of law."

It was brought by SNCC Mississippi Project director Robert Moses, Aaron Henry, Dave Dennis and Hunter Morey.

They contend that the people they represent "have been and will continue to be arrested, incarcerated, tried and convicted without due process of

CONTINUED ON PAGE 4

# DEMO CONVENTION FACES SHOWDOWN

MORE THAN 800 DELEGATES OF the Freedom Democratic Party from over 40 counties met in Jackson to choose 68 delegates and alternates to the National Democratic Convention.

### BOYCOTT THREATENED

ATLANTIC CITY, N. J. - "A proven lawless element is attempting to blackmail the President into preventing the seating of the Mississippi Freedom Democratic Party (FDP) delegation," an FDP spokesman said.

The spokesman was referring to a meeting of the governors of Mississippi, Alabama, Arkansas, Louisiana and Florida in New Orleans. They announced that if the Freedom delegation is seated their states would boycott the convention.

"It is horrible to think that the President would submit to political blackmail, especially by men who have defied the Federal government and one who is under indictment for criminal contempt," the spokesman continued.

### STATE BANS FDP

Meanwhile Mississippi State Chancery Judge Stokes Robertson, Jr. issued an injunction banning the operation of the Mississippi Freedom Democratic Party.

The suit, filed by State Attorney General J. T. Patterson, banned the FDP from acting as representatives of a "pretended political party" in Mississippi.

Patterson's suit charged that last week's state convention of the Freedom Democrats was designed to "intimidate and embarrass the lawfully existing Democratic Party and to create confusion in the minds of the electorate and bitterness, hatred and discord among the citizens."

Named as defendants were Aaron Henry, Rev. R.T. Smith, Mrs. Victoria Gray, Mrs. Fannie Lou Hamer, Lawrence Guyot, Leslie McLemore, Miss Peggy Connor, Rev. Ed King and Dr. A. D. Biettel.

Robertson's injunction barred the Freedom Party from using the name "Democratic."

### FDP CONVENTION HELD

Over 800 delegates attended the state convention of the Freedom Democratic party in Jackson Aug. 6. The participants elected 68 delegates and alternates to the national convention in Atlantic City. Aaron Henry heads the delegation while Mrs. Fannie Lou Hamer is vice-chairman. Rev. Ed King and Mrs. Victoria Gray were elected National Committeeman and Committeewoman. Lawrence Guyot will head the state executive committee.

The first four mentioned have been unsuccessful candidates in CONTINUED ON PAGE 4

The Student Voice, SNCC, vol. 5, no. 21, August 19, 1964

62

# CHAPTER TWELVE

# August 7, 1964

Rita and the Schwerners wanted Mickey to be buried side by side with James in Meridian, but the black undertaker refused for fear that his license would be revoked or worse. Several white undertakers were contacted, but none of them was willing to transport Mickey's body to a Negro cemetery. The autopsies had revealed that James had been severely beaten before he was shot. Other reports later claimed that the bulldozer had shattered his bones.

On Friday, August 7, James was buried in a private ceremony for immediate family and close friends. Ben's mood alternated between sorrow and rage. On the way to the funeral he muttered, "I'm gonna kill 'em!"

*Philadelphia, MS: Ben Chaney leans against his mother at the funeral of James Chaney.*

As he watched his brother's casket being lowered into the ground he shouted, "I want my brother! I want my brother!"

That night about two hundred people gathered at various churches in Meridian and marched to First Union Baptist Church for the memorial service. Many Freedom Summer workers took part. "I have been on a large number of walks, marches, vigils, pickets, etc., in my life," wrote a volunteer, "but I can't remember anything which was quite like this one. . . . It was completely silent . . . even though it lasted over 50 minutes, and even though there were a fair number of children involved."

*Dave Dennis delivering a eulogy for James Chaney*

At 7:30 p.m. hundreds of people crowded the church and sang "We Shall Overcome." Ben, crying, sat in the front row and leaned against his mother's shoulder.

COFO chairman Dave Dennis saw Ben's tears and scrapped the speech he was going to give for the eulogy. Instead, he began by saying, "I am not here to memorialize James Chaney, I am not here to pay tribute. . . . As I stand here I not only blame the people who pulled the trigger or did the beating or dug the hole with the shovel, I blame the people in Washington, D.C., and on down in the state of Mississippi for what happened."

As he spoke the mourners responded with shouts of *"Yes!" "That's right!" "Amen!"*

"What I want to talk about right now," said Dennis, "is the living dead that we have right among our midst, not only in the state of Mississippi but throughout the nation. Those are the people who *don't care.*"

Dennis recalled numerous cases of young black men and women who had been beaten and murdered, and their killers never brought to trial and allowed to go free. "I know what's going to happen," he said, speaking of Mickey, James, and Andrew. "When they find the people who killed these guys in Neshoba County, you've got to come back to the state of Mississippi and have a jury of their cousins, their aunts, and their uncles. And I know what they're going to say—not guilty. . . . I'm tired of that."

*"Yes, God help us! I am, too!"* responded the mourners.

"And one thing that I'm worried about," Dennis said, his voice rising, "is just exactly what are we going to do as people as a result of what happened, for what this guy died for and the other people died for?

"The best thing we can do for Mr. Chaney, for Mickey Schwerner, for Andrew Goodman is stand up and *demand* our rights!"

Dennis's eyes filled with tears. "We want our freedom now, *now*! I don't want to go to another memorial. I'm tired of *funerals*!" He banged his fist on the podium. "We've got to stand up."

He pleaded with the audience to register to vote and to get their neighbors registered. "Go down and do it! . . . Hold your heads up!"

"Dave finally broke down and couldn't finish," wrote Martha Honey, who was attending the service with her group from Mileston. She sat on the floor because the church was so packed.

"The Chaney family was moaning and much of the audience and I was also crying," said Martha. "Suddenly again, as I'd first realized when I heard the three men were missing when we were still training up at Oxford, I felt the sacrifice the Negroes have been making for so long."

After the service Martha and her group of white women and black men rode back to Mileston through the Delta in integrated cars. "White thugs" drove ahead of them and behind them making obscene gestures. "They tried to push us off the road," said Martha. "I was scared. It was ludicrous in a way."

Another student volunteer kept thinking about Dennis's words that evening and wrote, "As I was riding on the bus back to Laurel from Meridian after the service, all this kept running through my brain, along with the fact of knowing that nobody has ever been brought to justice in Mississippi for all those murders."

On Sunday, August 9, a funeral for Andrew was held at Ethical Culture Hall in New York, in the neighborhood where he had grown up. Every seat in the auditorium was taken. An overflow of several hundred mourners filled the basement, and more crowded the sidewalk outside. Andrew's parents and his brothers Jonathan and David sat in the front row beside the Chaney and Schwerner families.

The last speaker was Rabbi Arthur J. Lelyveld, a friend of the Goodman family. He had gone to Mississippi that summer as a representative of the National Council of Churches, and had been beaten over the head with a lead pipe by white ruffians. Rabbi Lelyveld said, "The tragedy of Andy Goodman cannot be separated from the tragedy of mankind. Along with James Chaney and Michael Schwerner, he has become the eternal evocation of all the host of beautiful young men and women who are carrying forward the struggle for which they gave their lives."

At the end of the service an usher removed the single yellow rose resting on top of Andrew's coffin and gave it to Carolyn Goodman. She linked arms with Fannie Lee Chaney and Anne Schwerner, and the three mothers, weeping, their heads bowed, walked out of the auditorium together as the mourners softly sang "We Shall Overcome."

That evening most of the same people attended services for Mickey at the Community Church in New York. The roster of speakers included Dave Dennis. Again he spoke angrily, as he had at James's memorial service. Like Rita, he believed that the national reaction to the murders demonstrated racism in America. A white life was considered more valuable than a black one. Dennis repeated his remarks that the murders would have probably gone unnoticed if two of the victims had not been white. "They were not the first to be killed in Mississippi," he said to the mourners. "I feel they are not going to be the last."

# CHAPTER THIRTEEN
# August 10, 1964

When the three bodies were recovered, Fannie Lee Chaney said, "I want everyone to know everything possible about what happened. . . . It is even more important now that the guilty ones be brought to trial and justice and be punished."

Inspector Sullivan focused on finding the person who had told the informant, Mr. X, where the bodies were buried. Sullivan knew that each man involved in the killings would suspect the other of ratting out to the FBI for money, so he and his team kept questioning key suspects.

Olen Burrage, who owned Old Jolly Farm, claimed he knew nothing about the three bodies. He told the *New York Times* that he had no idea how the bodies got there. "I want people to know I'm sorry it happened," he said. "I just don't know why anybody would kill them, and I don't believe in anything like that."

Years later Jerry Mitchell, a reporter for the *Clarion-Ledger* of Jackson, called Burrage and asked him what everybody wondered: "How could a bunch of Klansmen have slipped onto your property in the dead of night, run a bulldozer and buried three bodies fifteen feet down without you hearing or knowing something?"

Burrage hung up.

FBI agents asked Sheriff Rainey for another interview. Rainey insisted on seeing a search warrant. The agents said they didn't have one. Rainey told them to come back when they did. He told reporters that the FBI was hounding him. "The first we ever knew about the bodies being found was when we saw a television bulletin," he lied.

Klan conspirators were becoming increasingly jittery. Whoever had tipped off Mr. X might reveal more details about the crime. All the data gathered

HEAR! HEAR!
HOW OUR BROTHERS
Died For Freedom
AND HOW WE ARE CARRYING
ON THE FIGHT IN MISSISSIPPI

Mickey Schwerner    James Chaney    Andrew Goodman

HEAR
**Mrs. Fanny Chaney**
Courageous Mother of James Chaney
At New Zion Baptist Church
2319 THIRD STREET
THURS., AUG. 27, 1964
7:30 P. M.
CORE

*CORE poster publicizing a meeting featuring James Chaney's mother*

by the FBI was kept in a file with the code name "Mississippi Burning," or MIBURN. The file contained thousands of pages of interview summaries, maps, statistics, and sketches. However, Inspector Sullivan and J. Edgar Hoover refused to turn the file over to the state of Mississippi.

"We could not trust the state to do the right thing with the information," said the FBI. Mississippi had never convicted a white person of killing a black person. If the federal government was going to indict and try the men who had murdered Mickey, James, and Andrew, it would have to be on a charge of violating their civil rights.

President Johnson at his Texas ranch predicted "substantive results" in the murder case. Reporters rushed to Philadelphia expecting arrests to be made momentarily.

Preparations were under way for the Neshoba County Fair, known as "Mississippi's Giant Houseparty." Dating back to 1889, the fair offered a week of socializing and entertainment: livestock exhibits, beauty pageants, rides, games, barbecues, and country music. During the celebration it was a custom for white people to stay in cabins on the fairgrounds that had belonged to their families for generations.

But the campsite was located two miles from Old Jolly Farm. The FBI had set up roadblocks around that area to keep sightseers away. And the horror of the crime overshadowed the festivities.

Jim Dees, who was ten, remembered the FBI searching the campsite for additional clues the week before the fair started. "The fact is, Neshoba County . . . will forever have those images associated with it," he said. "Every time CNN, or whomever runs a profile, the grainy black-and-white footage of troups and bayonets or the three forlorn faces pop up. It's our history, and we, as Mississippians, have to as they say nowadays 'own it.'"

The fair opened on Monday, August 10, in a tense, gloomy mood. Politicians who were supposed to speak canceled their appearances. Instead, Governor Paul Johnson gave a speech praising the "law-abiding" people of Neshoba County and blasting Freedom Summer. "We will not permit outsiders to subvert our people and our rights," he said. "Segregation is the only way to peace and harmony between the races." Thousands cheered.

A small airplane dropped leaflets from the Ku Klux Klan claiming that Mickey, James, and Andrew were "Communist Revolutionaries, actively working to undermine and destroy Christian Civilization."

The Freedom Summer workers also passed out leaflets. Theirs were song sheets, or information about voting. Many of the black men and women who received the fliers couldn't read. Some said, "I just can't get my mind on all that. I just never voted and I'm too old now."

Others had a raft of excuses:

"I don't want to mess with that mess."

"I don't have the time."

*A voter registration team at work in Drew, MS*

*Mrs. Hamer instructing voter applicants*

"I got to think about it."

"I can't sign no paper."

"Been advised not to register."

"Satisfied with things as they are."

Freedom Summer workers refused to give up. Out on the plantations, which were owned by whites, the volunteers had to sneak in at dawn or at night.

"Volunteers had to take their clipboards out at 3 a.m. to catch the plantation buses and sign up the riders," wrote Sally Belfrage.

They did their best, but had to be careful. "Many plantations—homes included—are posted, meaning that no trespassing is permitted," wrote Joel, a volunteer in Mileston. "We're especially concerned with the number of roads in and out. . . . For instance, some houses could be too dangerous to canvas because of their location near the boss man's house and on a dead end road."

One out of twenty people might be convinced to register. Mrs. Hamer insisted that people go to the courthouse with the volunteers before she would give them the shirts, dresses, and pants that had been donated by Northern supporters. "The women were scared to death but they were motivated by Mrs. Hamer," said a SNCC staffer. "They wanted the clothing."

"Mrs. Hamer was one of the smartest women I've ever known," said Linda Davis, a volunteer in Ruleville. "She could persuade others to register to vote."

Mrs. Hamer's power to win over potential voters was famous. She once interrupted a nutrition class at the Ruleville Freedom School, and convinced the thirty women to pile into volunteers' cars and try to register.

At a mass meeting in Sunflower County, she rose to speak and "an electric atmosphere suffused the entire church," remembered Robert Jackall, a young professor at Georgetown University. "Men and women alike began to stand up, to call out her name, and to urge her on. . . . She ended by leading the assembly in chorus after chorus of a rousing old Negro spiritual called, appropriately, 'This Little Light of Mine.' "

Many came to the meetings just to enjoy the singing. Rev. Aaron Johnson, who opened his church for a meeting, said, "People were afraid to come at first, but when they did, we rocked the church. Tonight I said, 'Well, if I die, I had a good time tonight. I had a *good* time tonight.'"

Civil rights leaders were song leaders. Sam Block, who had been involved in the movement since he was a teenager, said, "I began to see the music itself as an important organizing tool to really bring people together—not only to bring them together but to hold them together. I started to give people the responsibility of thinking about a song that they would want to sing that night and of changing that song, you know, from a gospel song."

At the first mass meeting at Williams Chapel in Ruleville, Charles McLaurin took charge and let the volunteers in his group introduce themselves. Then he led the audience in singing "Go Tell It on the Mountain!"

"Tomorra [sic] we start signing folks up here in Ruleville," he said. "We're gonna knock on every door. And then we're goin' into Drew, and Shaw, even Indianola."

Everybody surged up the aisles, clapping and singing:

*Ain't gonna let no-body turn me round,*
*Turn me round,*
*Turn me round,*
*Ain't gonna let no-body turn me round.*

*Children on a porch in Ruleville*

*Canton residents waiting to take the voter registration oath before a federal registrar*

# CHAPTER FOURTEEN
# Mid-August 1964

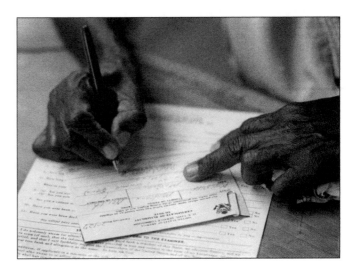

*A black citizen fills out a voter registration form before a federal registrar, Canton.*

The most important goal of Freedom Summer was getting black people to go to the courthouse to register to vote. However, even after people were persuaded to register, they faced enormous obstacles. "I was working mostly with black women who had found the courage to go all the way down to the county seat in Indianola to try to register," said Linda Davis. "Many of them had made that trip of thirty miles more than *twenty* times. And each and every time they had been refused by the white registrar of voters."

"From 1956 to 1963 only seven black people in Sunflower County had registered," said Mrs. Bernice White, a college-educated science teacher. She first tried in 1956. The circuit clerk said to her, "Come back in March." Mrs. White went back in March and the clerk said, "We're not voting here. Go down to City Hall."

In 1963 Mrs. White said to her husband, "Maybe we need to start help changing ways." The next week she took her twin daughters with her when she went to the courthouse. "You can't take those young 'uns in there," said the clerk. When she got home Mr. White told her to leave the children with her aunt the next time she tried to register.

Mrs. White returned to the courthouse but the clerk said there were too many people coming at once and they could handle only one and two at a time. "I was by myself, and I was really not afraid," Mrs. White recalled. "I was angry, more angry than I was anything. . . . And I think it's out of anger how I got involved in voter's rights."

*Organizers Doug Smith (left) and Sandy Leigh (far right) explain voter registration procedures to 103-year-old Felix Smith on his front porch.*

The next time she tried to register the clerk gave her thirty-seven questions. "And, of course, I was given a Constitution book and told what page and what section to interpret," she said. Blacks were required to read and interpret part of the Mississippi Constitution, which contained 285 sections. Each interpretive essay would be judged by the local registrar as passing or failing.

When Mrs. White was almost finished the registrar said, "You've got to go. We've got to close this place up." "He didn't close it up till I turned my paper in," said Mrs. White, "and he told me to come back in two weeks."

When she and her husband returned they were not told whether they had passed the test. The registrar just said, "Sign the book."

Later Mrs. White testified on behalf of the United States in an important civil rights case, United States of America vs. C. C. Campbell, et. al., about the discrimination she had experienced.

Although many, like Mr. and Mrs. White, tried to register, few succeeded. SNCC staffers had been giving classes to teach black people how to pass the literacy test before Freedom Summer began, and now they trained the volunteers as teachers.

"The voter registration classes are slightly tense, but what is more present is hope," wrote a volunteer in McComb. "The people dress up carefully. They shake each other's hands, await eagerly the return of those who have gone down to the courthouse already."

For some, even the act of trying to register was enlightening. A cotton picker named Unita Blackwell attended a church rally in Issaquena County. When the leader asked for volunteers to take the voter registration test, she was one of five women and three men who went to the courthouse. Later she said, "I was just starting to learn about myself and history in a brand-new way."

Freedom School teachers canvassed door-to-door on the weekends. Canvassers were often followed by threatening police in cars inching alongside them, displaying guns. Dozens of volunteers were arrested for passing out voting material. "Canvassing is dirty work," wrote a volunteer. "It is very tiring, and frankly boring after the first hour or so. . . . It is almost impossible to overcome the fears. . . . And the courthouse people make sure you have to wait a long time."

A volunteer named Bill who was working in Greenwood wrote, "Three different cars tried to run me down when I was in a parking lot of a large supermarket registering people."

Martha Honey in Mileston remembered "going down red dirt roads, corn growing on either side," and stopping at "poor houses."

*Sunday school in Ruleville*

*After a cross was burned in front of an Indianola Freedom House, it was turned into a freedom sign.*

"People wouldn't come to the door," she said. "They were so scared, and rightfully so. Some people would latch the door when you came around. Others would be quaking because there was a white at the door." If they did open the door, Martha would say, "Come down to the courthouse and register to vote." And sometimes they'd say yes.

Canvassers were trained to jump into ditches alongside the roads to hide when cars came by that might be driven by attackers armed with weapons. Once Martha was canvassing with a teen student who later became the first black mayor of his town. They were walking along when a car approached and they "hit the ditch."

On weekdays Freedom School teachers continued working with kids as young as three and four, as well as adults. A thousand students had been expected; two thousand enrolled. Originally the plan was to have twenty-five schools serving tenth- and eleventh-grade students. By the end of the summer, there were fifty schools scattered throughout Mississippi with 2,500 students ranging in age from preschool to seniors. Some schools were in shacks, others in church basements or on lawns under the trees.

Jo in Canton wrote that her group created a Freedom School in a one-room wooden church that had been bombed out in June. At first nobody came to classes out of fear. "The police have been circling it [the church] hourly since we moved into it," she wrote. But gradually people showed up, "20 a day now—never the same 20."

Len Edwards wrote to a friend, "Our community in Ruleville is the most joyful group you could imagine. All activity is around the Freedom School and community center. There all day long children and adults from the Negro community come in and go to classes, sing songs and learn with the white teachers who are down here. The place buzzes with activity."

Almost every Freedom School published a newspaper featuring students' poems, essays, and drawings. Kids wrote short stories about their lives. Some heard the poetry of Langston Hughes and felt inspired.

Edith Moore, age fifteen, in McComb, wrote:

*Isn't it awful not to be able to eat in a public place*
*Without being arrested or snarled at right in your face?*

Allan Goodner in Clarksdale wrote:

*Segregation will not be here long*
*I will do my best to see it gone.*

*Meridian Freedom Summer sample class/attendance chart*

*Local children making freedom chains at community center, Clarksdale*

Students discussed civil rights, and the origin of slavery in America, and the role of Negroes in the American Revolution. Walter Saddler, a teenager attending a Freedom School in Gluckstadt, developed an interest in "Negro history."

"It was something new to me," he wrote, "and it really taught me a lot." After the Gluckstadt school was burned down he attended a Freedom School in Canton in the fall. Walter went to classes at the end of his regular school day and hoped to go to college. "I know I could do a good job," he wrote. And he did. Ten years later Walter Saddler became the anchor on Mississippi's most popular television news program.

Pamela Parker in Holly Springs wrote, "The atmosphere in class is unbelievable. It is what every teacher dreams about—real, honest enthusiasm and desire to learn anything and everything. . . . I have a great deal of faith in these students. . . . I really think that they will be able to carry on without us."

*Freedom School student Pat Thompson at work on an art project*

*Freedom School students at Mt. Zion Baptist Church, Hattiesburg*

# CHAPTER FIFTEEN

# August 16, 1964

As Freedom Summer drew to a close, one hundred students from Freedom Schools across the state gathered for a convention in Meridian to demonstrate what they had been learning.

Bob Moses attended the conference and seemed gratified as he observed committees of young black people discussing slum clearance, an end to the poll tax, and equal housing for blacks. The students even declared a new Declaration of Independence "from the unjust laws of Mississippi."

"It was the single time I have seen Bob the happiest," said an observer. "He just thought this was what it was all about."

When reporters asked Moses to comment on the success of the Summer Project, he said, "Success? I have trouble with that word. When we started we hoped no one would be killed."

On August 16, a memorial service was held for the three civil rights workers at the burned-out remains of Mount Zion Methodist Church at Longdale. People sat on wooden benches among the trees. Sheriff Rainey and Deputy Price lurked nearby, watching and listening.

Ben Chaney made a speech and said, "I want us all to stand up here together and say just one thing. I want the sheriff to hear this good. *We ain't scared no more of Sheriff Rainey!*"

*Memorial service for James Chaney, Michael Schwerner, and Andrew Goodman at the site of the burned-down Mt. Zion Methodist Church in Longdale*

*Mrs. Fannie Lee Chaney speaks at the memorial service for her son James Chaney.*

His mother, Mrs. Chaney, said, "When my child drove nights out here to this church, who grudged him so much that they thought they had to kill him? Mickey Schwerner, he was like a son of mine. James said, 'Mama, that man's got sense. He's down here to help us. . . . I'm going with him.' That was my child as well as Mickey and Andy. And I just don't want those children's work to be in vain."

Bob Moses also spoke. He said, "The problem of Mississippi is the problem of the nation and of the world. A way has to be found to change this desire to kill."

Inspector Sullivan and his men were aggressively pursuing their inquiries in Neshoba County, determined to crack the case. Evidence revealed that the

*Bob Moses at the memorial service for Chaney, Schwerner, and Goodman on the ruins of Mt. Zion Methodist Church in Longdale*

victims had been shot at close range, which meant they were probably held captive up until their deaths.

Klansmen were on alert and suspended some of their usual terrorist activities. They were aware that any crime they committed would be investigated immediately. Nevertheless COFO reported continued beatings, shootings, arrests, churches burned to the ground, and cars damaged and destroyed.

SNCC leaders wondered what Freedom Summer had really accomplished. The main goal had been voter registration, yet this had not yet been achieved in significant numbers. The National Democratic Convention was going to be held at the end of August in Atlantic City, New Jersey. Moses wanted to send a delegation including and representing blacks as well as whites, the Mississippi Freedom Democratic Party.

The MFDP would challenge and perhaps unseat the "official" all-white delegation from Mississippi. The founders of the MFDP needed their own party because the Mississippi Democratic Party controlled the state legislature that had passed laws making the registration process almost impossible for blacks. Its 1964 platform stated, "The separation of the races is necessary for the peace and tranquility of all the people of Mississippi."

The MFDP had been formed in March 1964. The party was open to "all Mississippians," said Mrs. Hamer, "white, black, brown, cream, or polka dot." She had run for Congress in the June primary. "I'm showing the people that a Negro can run for office." But she had been defeated by the white incumbent in her district. Now Mrs. Hamer and the party set their sights on Atlantic City.

Mr. Oscar Giles, owner of the Penny Saver grocery store in Indianola, became involved in the MFDP and was chosen as one of the delegates. His son Eugene, then nine years old, rode to the meetings with him. "I used to go to Mrs. Hamer's house in Ruleville several times," he remembered. "They were doing the organizing. I understood most definitely what was going on." When Mr. Giles and his son left Mrs. Hamer's house after a meeting they found threatening notes

*Mr. and Mrs. Oscar Giles in Giles Grocery, Indianola*

on their car. But Mr. Giles wouldn't let his son read the notes. "He protected us from bad language. We weren't allowed to curse," Dr. Giles recalled.

"Dad didn't trust the mail service [in Indianola]. He wrote letters to the Justice Department, anyone who would listen, and he and I would drive to Mound Bayou [thirty-seven miles away] to mail them."

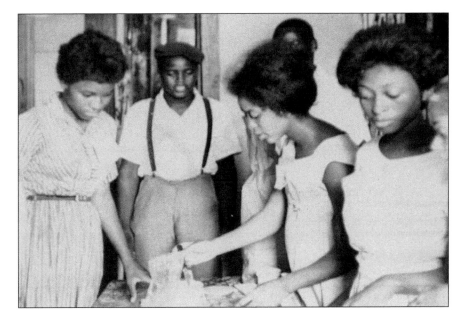

Bernice and Artie Sims (right) at the Statewide Mississippi Freedom School Convention in the Meridian Baptist Seminary building

Dr. Giles said to his father, "Why do we have to go all the way to Mound Bayou?"

Mr. Giles said, "I can be assured the letter will get out."

For a show of strength the MFDP had to have the names of Mississippians signed up as Freedom Democrats. Moses hoped for four hundred thousand signatures. By August he had only 21,421, so he called upon Freedom Summer volunteers to pitch in. Moses issued an emergency memo: "*Everyone* who is not working in Freedom Schools or community centers *must* devote all their time to organizing for the convention challenge."

Volunteers went to shacks and out to the cotton fields to encourage black people to sign up to join the new party.

"No, there's no danger in signing *this* paper."

"Your name will not be listed in any newspaper."

"The boss man will never know what the MFDP is. What is it? Here's a brochure."

And the brochure explained the process. Volunteers went to juke joints and churches to get signatures. On Sunday mornings they waited till after the collection plate went around, then they explained the Freedom Democratic Party and the convention.

Moses and SNCC leaders needed money to send the MFDP delegates to Atlantic City, so they asked black celebrity entertainers for help. Harry Belafonte, the famed Calypso singer, had been raising money on the East Coast. When the bodies of Mickey, James, and Andy were found and made headlines, money poured in. Belafonte had too much to safely wire to Mississippi. On August 16 he and Sidney Poitier, the first black actor to win an

Oscar, flew into Greenwood, Mississippi, and brought a satchel containing seventy thousand dollars in cash. SNCC leaders were on the tarmac to welcome them, and drove them to town in a convoy. Klansmen were there, too, in pickup trucks, and chased the cars through cotton fields. They rammed the car holding Belafonte and Poitier, then pulled alongside threateningly. Belafonte's heart was pounding in terror. For Poitier it was a "nerve-wracking experience" that he later said enabled him to play a police detective forced to help solve a crime in a racist Southern Mississippi town in his now famous movie *In the Heat of the Night*.

When the convoy finally reached the Elks Hall, the Klansmen turned back. Crowds cheered the two stars and shouted, "Freedom! Freedom! Freedomfreedomfreedomfreedom!"

"Sydney and I had heard a lot of applause in our day," said Belafonte, "but never anything like those cheers."

Poitier stepped to the podium and said tearfully, "I have been a lonely man all my life until I came to Greenwood, Mississippi. I have been lonely because I have not found love, but this room is *overflowing* with it."

Then Belafonte sang "Day-O," his signature song, and the audience sang it as a civil rights anthem: "Freedom come an' it won't be long." He held up the satchel, turned it upside down over a table, and dumped out bundles of cash "to delirious shouts."

A volunteer named Bret who was in the audience wrote to his family about the evening. "It was a deeply exciting experience, and a strange and enlightening one. . . . We saw public figures become private ones, and we saw human beings informed more fully before us."

That night Belafonte and Poitier stayed in a house guarded by men with shotguns. Too frightened to sleep, they kept calm by doing calisthenics and telling each other ghost stories. The next morning they flew back to New York City.

Some entertainers promised to come to Mississippi but backed out because they were afraid. However, folk singer Pete Seeger appeared twice. He admired Bob Moses and "came down to help."

"The African tradition of singing was stronger in this movement," said Seeger. "Armies use music to whip up enthusiasm for battle. You don't feel quite so lonely. Group singing was a black tradition in the South.

"But surely there never was a movement like the civil rights movement to make music such a central part of its meetings, rallies, marches, sit-ins, mass imprisonments.

"White people latched on to freedom songs and Afro-American songs."

When Seeger gave an outdoor concert in McComb behind the Freedom House, he sang "Abiyoyo" and "What a Beautiful City." Dozens of black kids

were there along with volunteers like Ira Landess. Landess noticed two white teenagers standing by themselves. He went over to talk to them and they said they had come to hear Seeger. One of the teens, Gary Brooks, had started to explore the black part of town on the other side of the railroad tracks. He had just read *Black Like Me,* a book by white journalist John Howard Griffin recording his experiences passing as a black man on a six-month tour through the South in 1959. At the end of the concert the boys said they would continue their conversation with Landess, and they soon phoned him at the Freedom House to arrange another meeting. During the rest of the summer they kept dropping by the Freedom House, and Landess warmly welcomed them.

Black folksinger Julius Lester did concerts, too. "Ain't Gonna Let Nobody Turn Me 'Round' was generally the third song I would do," he said, "because it was easily adaptable to any town with the names of the local mayor, sheriff, etc., being substituted for 'nobody.' I remember one night in Meridian, Mississippi . . . I led this song for half an hour with people in

*Pete Seeger performing at the Palmer's Crossing community center, Hattiesburg*

*Julius Lester
performing
at Mt. Zion
Baptist Church,
Hattiesburg*

the audience putting in names of who or what was not going to turn them around."

During his tour Lester slept in his car and was reported as "feeling death all around him."

"Each morning I wake thinking today I die," he wrote in his journal. Yet when he returned to New York he convinced other singers to come south.

Bluesmen Muddy Waters and Mississippi John Hurt also performed. Between songs they discussed the black contribution to American music. And afterward they sang with volunteers and locals till after midnight.

The blues had been born in the Delta. B. B. King, the son of sharecroppers in Berclair, had moved to Indianola as a teenager and considered it his hometown. He performed with a gospel quartet over the radio on Sunday mornings. But on Saturday nights he stayed at a café owned by Stacy White's grandfather that was open all night. "My grandfather would feed him," said Stacy, and King played songs.

Throughout August the Free Southern Theater gave performances in Freedom Schools and at community centers. The group had been founded at Tougaloo College in Jackson. It was the first integrated live theater group in the South. Its play *In White America* by Martin Duberman dramatized race relations starting with slavery and closing with the lynching of Mickey, James, and Andy. If Rita was present she gave a speech at the end.

When the theater company first toured Mississippi and performed in McComb, a bomb was thrown near the stage. Everyone scattered. But when the smoke cleared people returned. No one was hurt, and the actors continued their performance. "I was afraid but so was everyone," said Denise Nicholas, a black member of the company from Ann Arbor, Michigan.

In Mileston they gave the show in a half-built community center, a gift from Abe Osheroff, a Southern California carpenter. "We sang to the heavens, to the trees, to the air," recalled Denise. "We harvested hope everywhere we went."

In Ruleville the troupe performed Samuel Beckett's *Waiting for Godot*, about two characters waiting for someone named Godot to come and save them. Mrs. Hamer attended and shouted, "We been waitin' and waitin'!"

"She brought that play home to our audience," said Denise.

When they gave Gil Moses' play *Roots* in a tiny church, Denise was having trouble with one of the props during a scene. "A man came quietly up onto the stage from the audience to help me open a jar I was trying to open," she recalled. "It was the kindest gesture."

The troupe did a notable production of *Purlie Victorious*, a comedy by Ossie Davis. They staged the play in an open field after local segregationists burned down the church where they were supposed to perform. "We developed improvisational pieces involving the local people and their struggles in a particular town," said Denise. "These pieces were miracles. The audiences reveled in seeing themselves and their plight up on the stage nearly overnight."

One volunteer took a group of Freedom School kids to Biloxi for a performance of *In White America* and heard Rita speak. "It is pretty strong stuff," wrote the volunteer. "This was the first theater most of these people had ever seen. They didn't have theater manners and it was great."

Audiences stomped, clapped, and clamored for more. As if in church, they shouted "That's right!" and "Tell it!"

One of the actresses in the play said, "You can't imagine what it was like under slavery," and a fifteen-year-old girl in the audience said, "Oh, yes I can."

*Mrs. Hamer at the MFDP delegates challenge, Atlantic City, NJ*

# CHAPTER SIXTEEN

# Late August, 1964

The work that Bob Moses had urged the volunteers to do for the Mississippi Freedom Democratic Party paid off. On August 19 the MFDP delegation was heading for the Democratic National Convention in Atlantic City. Black people of Mississippi wanted to represent themselves and be heard. Before Freedom Summer began they had been shut out of the county conventions that chose the "official" delegation, all whites. Now the Freedom Democrats were going to challenge them and ask to be seated at the convention.

That evening three buses lined up in front of the COFO office on Lynch Street in Jackson. An integrated group of sixty-seven Freedom Democrats (regular delegates and alternates) boarded the bus as crowds cheered and sang "We Shall Overcome." The delegates and twenty-eight alternates included sharecroppers, barbers, maids, and cooks: Miss Peggy Jean Connor, who owned a beauty shop in Hattiesburg; Oscar Giles, the owner of Giles Penny Saver grocery store in Indianola; Miss Unita Blackwell, the cotton picker from Issaquena County who had recently gone to her first meeting and had become involved in the MFDP; two sons of slaves; and four white men. Most of these people had never been out of Mississippi before. The buses pulled out at 10 p.m. and everyone broke into freedom songs.

Civil rights leaders such as Mrs. Hamer, Charles McLaurin, Miss Ella Baker, Aaron Henry, Leslie McLemore, Ed King, and Lawrence Guyot were also selected for the MFDP delegation. Guyot had been elected as the party's chair, but he was being held in the Hattiesburg jail, having been convicted on false charges.

In Atlantic City the delegates and alternates checked into the Gem Hotel and shared rooms. McLemore had been in Washington and was already there. McLaurin met them at the hotel, too. Chris Williams, a volunteer,

*Bob Moses, probably on the convention floor in Atlantic City, NJ*

drove up in his car to help. "A number of Freedom volunteers were working with us," said Dr. McLemore, who later became a professor of political science. Chris and many other Freedom Summer volunteers manned the phones at the hotel and handed out booklets reporting crimes against blacks as well as the murders of Mickey, James, and Andrew.

Mrs. Hamer had been in New York to speak at a meeting. On Saturday afternoon, August 22, she joined the delegation and marched with them to the Convention Hall. From the Oval Office President Johnson agreed to let the Freedom Democrats make their challenge to the Credentials Committee. The event was televised nationally. Volunteers back in Mississippi gathered around TVs to watch.

Mrs. Hamer sat at the witness table and spoke. "It was the thirty-first of August in 1962 that eighteen of us traveled twenty-six miles to the county courthouse in Indianola to try to register to become first-class citizens," she said.

When she got home her boss, the owner of the Marlow plantation, said, "Fannie Lou, if you don't go down and withdraw your registration you will have to leave."

"Mr. Marlow, I didn't try to register for you; I tried to register for myself," she told the committee. "I had to leave that same night."

All of a sudden the networks interrupted their convention coverage and switched to the White House. President Johnson gave a press conference, purposely cutting into Mrs. Hamer's testimony. He worried that she would gain the sympathy of the committee and American viewers, which would hurt his reelection in the South. By the time TV coverage returned to Atlantic City, Mrs. Hamer had finished and Rita Schwerner was testifying.

But that evening Mrs. Hamer's entire speech was replayed on all the networks. She told how she had been arrested in Winona, Mississippi, carried to the county jail, and savagely beaten for participating in voter registration. "They beat me and they beat me with the long, flat blackjack," she said, weeping.

Committee members also were crying. McLaurin, too.

"All of this is on account of we want to register, to become first-class citizens," said Mrs. Hamer. "Just taking a chance on trying to register to vote, you can be fired. Not only fired, you can be killed. You know it's true because you know what happened to Schwerner, Goodman, and Chaney. We need a change in the state of Mississippi. . . . And if the Freedom Democratic Party is not seated—*now*—*I question America. Is this America?*"

Within minutes telegrams flooded the White House demanding that the Freedom Party be seated at the convention. *Now!*

On Sunday two thousand supporters gathered on the Boardwalk outside the Convention Hall as Mrs. Hamer sang "This Little Light of Mine."

*Mrs. Hamer and MFDP delegates singing at a boardwalk rally in Atlantic City*

*Rita Schwerner and John Lewis listening to the MFDP testimony to the Credentials Committee*

On Monday MFDP supporters staged a sit-in. Silently they sat on the boardwalk and held signs that showed pictures of Mickey, James, and Andrew. Ben Chaney held the one with the portrait of his brother. A wrecked 1950s sedan was displayed on a trailer to represent the burned station wagon that the three civil rights workers had driven.

That afternoon members of the Credentials Committee met with black leaders. The committee offered the Freedom Democrats two seats at the convention instead of all sixty-eight. Mrs. Hamer said, "We didn't come all this way for no two seats. All of us is tired."

On Tuesday the sit-in continued. Meanwhile the Credentials Committee approved the compromise, and it was adopted that evening at the convention.

During the speeches Freedom Democrats slipped into the Convention

Hall, making their presence known. Volunteers borrowed badges for them from the regular delegates so they could get in.

"I made four or five trips in and out—it was really exciting," wrote a volunteer. "I felt like Mata Hari and the French Resistance and the Underground Railroad all rolled into one. . . . We got lots of sympathy and we didn't compromise ourselves by accepting a phony compromise."

On Wednesday the MFDP voted on the compromise. A few approved it. Mrs. Hamer and the majority did not, and the party rejected the offer.

The following night President Johnson appeared at the convention to accept the Democratic nomination. Outside, Mrs. Hamer led the Freedom Democrats and volunteers in singing "Go Tell It on the Mountain."

The next morning she and the disappointed delegates boarded the buses to return to Mississippi. When asked why she persisted in her struggle for civil rights, she said, "All my life I've been sick and tired. Now I'm sick and tired of being sick and tired."

The MFDP was already planning a new campaign, a Freedom Vote in November to show that masses of blacks wanted to vote. Some Freedom Summer workers stayed to help.

"Dear Family," wrote Gene, a volunteer in Batesville. "I must tell you that I am reconsidering my decision to return to school this fall. . . . The question of continuing my work in Mississippi has been on my mind. . . . My involvement here is quite deep. . . . I can see a job that needs to be done and I can do it."

A volunteer named Tommy remained in Philadelphia, "the town of death," where Mickey, James, and Andrew had been murdered. He wrote to his parents, "I only know that I must carry on this struggle that other people have died in, and that someday the system will be changed."

# CHAPTER SEVENTEEN

# Aftermath

"The killers who murdered Andy and Mickey and James are still out there, uncaught and unindicted," wrote Tracy Sugarman in his log when he left Mississippi at the end of Freedom Summer.

Then, during the second week of September 1964, the FBI got a break in the case. Klansman Wallace Miller, a policeman, told agents that at a Klan gathering in May it was decided to "get Goatee [Mickey]." Mount Zion Church had been burned to lure Mickey back to Neshoba County. The execution had been planned by the Klan's imperial wizard, Sam Bowers, and Edgar Ray Killen, known as "The Preacher." Miller also spilled names of others involved.

FBI agents tracked down James Jordan in Gulfport, Louisiana, on October 13. Jordan confessed in exchange for $3,500 and help in relocating him and his family. He said that Preacher Killen had rounded up the lynch mob when Mickey, James, and Andrew were in jail. Jordan named seventeen conspirators including Deputy Price and Sheriff Rainey. However, he claimed that he had not been one of the killers.

On November 19 and 20 the FBI questioned Horace Doyle Barnette. Barnette admitted that he had witnessed the murders, and reported that Wayne Roberts had shot Mickey and Andrew, and Jordan had killed James.

Armed with the confessions of eyewitnesses, the Justice Department prepared its case for a federal grand jury. The charge would be depriving others of their civil rights, based on a federal law dating back to 1870. On December 4, FBI agents arrested nineteen men.

The case went to trial in Meridian on October 7, 1967. The all-white jury found seven men guilty, and they were sentenced to terms of three to ten years in jail. Sheriff Rainey and Burrage, the owner of Old Jolly Farm, were acquitted. The jury was deadlocked on Killen because one juror said she "could never convict a preacher."

But in 1983 Neshoba County Klan Imperial Wizard Sam Halloway Bowers admitted that Killen, who had walked free, had been the main organizer of the murders. With this information the families of Mickey, James, and Andrew worked to reopen the case.

Ben Chaney told reporters, "There are many, many who are alive who should stand trial."

In 1999 the Mississippi attorney general began investigating. A journalist wrote about the case and dug up new evidence, and even discovered the identity of Mr. X. An Illinois high school teacher and his students helped the reporter as a project for History Day.

On January 6, 2005, the police finally arrested Killen and charged him with murder. The trial began on June 12. Rita, Carolyn Goodman, and Ben and Mrs. Chaney sat in the gallery. The women testified. Killen, eighty years old and in a wheelchair, pleaded not guilty.

On June 21 the jury reached a verdict. They found Killen guilty on three counts of manslaughter. The judge sentenced him to serve three twenty-year terms in jail.

The families of the victims hugged and cried.

When reporters asked Rita for comments she repeated a belief she had expressed during the search for the missing men: "You're treating this trial as the most important trial of the civil rights movement because two of the three men were white. That means we all have a discussion about racism in this country that has to continue."

It was said that Freedom Summer "changed Mississippi forever." SNCC compiled an assessment of the Freedom Summer Project's accomplishments (see Appendix B). Freedom Summer was one of the forces that led President Johnson to sign the Voting Rights Act into law on August 6, 1965. The legislation prohibited discriminatory voting practices such as literacy tests and poll taxes. As a result black voter registration in Mississippi soared. By the end of 1966 the number of eligible black voters who were registered had risen from 6.4 percent to nearly 60 percent.

In Philadelphia, where Mickey, James, and Andrew had been killed, black students returning to school wore buttons that read ONE MAN, ONE VOTE.

*Mississippi child*

*Lelia Jean
Waterhouse*

"Freedom Schools started a new way to educate people in local communities," said Dr. Leslie McLemore, a civil rights veteran and director of The Hamer Institute at Jackson State University.

Cephus Smith, a Ruleville teenager, said, "I'd never known any white kids before last summer. It meant somethin' to be around white kids—to be able to say what I wanted to say."

Host families sustained friendships with Freedom Summer volunteers. The Waterhouse girls kept up a correspondence with Andy Schiffrin, and Lelia Jean wrote about a group trip she had taken to New York and New Jersey: "We lived with a white family for the first five (5) days. . . . It was quite an experience to live with white families in the north. They don't consider race in some places up north." Lelia Jean also told Andy what was happening in Meridian: "24 students attempted to enroll in white schools, Sept 4, 1964, 1–6 Grade, including Ben Chaney. . . . I am going to enroll at an all white school I hope, along with some other children of high school age, so wish me luck. . . . I am still working at the Cofo [sic] office every day." In a PS she added, "I miss you very, very much. Wish you could come back."

Stacy White, now a computer science professor at Mississippi Valley State College, said, "Freedom Summer opened up doors for African Americans in the Delta. We have more elected officials than any state in the Union. It took all these years. The culmination is President Obama. If it weren't for Freedom Summer we wouldn't have President Obama."

Bob Moses gave credit to black grassroots leaders like Mrs. Hamer, who shaped the Southern civil rights movement as a whole. Mrs. Hamer said the Summer Project was "one of the greatest things that ever happened in Mississippi."

"There were people who wanted change, but they hadn't dared to come out and try to do something," she wrote. "But after the 1964 project when all of the young people came down for the summer, Negro people in the Delta began moving. . . . To me, the 1964 Summer Project was the beginning of a New Kingdom right here on earth. . . . James Chaney, Andrew Goodman, and Mickey Schwerner gave their lives that one day we would be free."

*Dr. Stacy White*

# The Story Continues. . . .

*"We own this country as much as anybody else." Charles McLaurin in Indianola*

Rita Schwerner Bender, now a lawyer specializing in family law, said, "We have to talk about the unfinished promise of the civil rights movement."

"The economic issues are still huge," noted Linda Davis, a retired superior court judge in the District of Columbia.

"Each generation has to pick up where the other one left off," said Charles McLaurin. "This one is better prepared."

The Sunflower County Civil Rights Organization meets once a month in Ruleville to discuss ongoing concerns. When I visited in 2013 the organization was planning a statewide 50th-anniversary of Freedom Summer. In Sunflower County the reunion celebration would feature a performance of the play *In White America*, panel discussions, singing, and a tour of civil rights landmarks such as the Fannie Lou Hamer Museum and Memorial Garden. For years, McLaurin has been giving tours of sites where civil rights history happened. Under consideration is the possibility of designating the Old Jail in Drew with a historical marker. McLaurin was imprisoned there and so were dozens of SNCC and COFO leaders and Freedom Summer volunteers.

The Sunflower organization partnered with the Samuel Proctor Oral History Program to collect testimonies that tell the Mississippi story so that these voices will not be forgotten.

"Education is the only way out of any type of poverty," said Mrs. Bernice White in an interview at Tougaloo College. The advice she gave to students was: "Don't depend on miracles. Education is a miracle."

"The Movement never stops," says McLaurin.

# Where to See More and Learn More About Freedom Summer

*Kathy Rubel in the Ruleville community center*

The Council of Federated Organizations (COFO), 1017 John R. Lynch Street, Jackson, Mississippi.

The Fannie Lou Hamer Museum and Memorial Garden, Ruleville, Mississippi.

The Hamer Institute at Jackson State University, Jackson, Mississippi.

The McCain Library and Archives, University of Southern Mississippi, Hattiesburg, Mississippi.

The Mississippi Department of Archives and History, Jackson, Mississippi.

Tougaloo College Archives, Jackson, Mississippi.

## Websites:

www.crmvet.org

www.digilib.usm.edu/cdm/singleitem/collection/usmfa/id/23/rec/1

www.loc.gov/folklife/civilrights/survey/view_collection.php?coll_id=1385

www.learntoquestion.com

www.wisconsinhistory.org

http://mlk-kpp01.standford.edu/

civil.rights@oberlin.edu

# TIME LINE

*Female student volunteer. "You've got to expect to be frightened."*

| | |
|---|---|
| **1961** | The Congress of Racial Equality (CORE) sponsors Freedom Rides, which are interracial sit-ins on bus trips across the South. |
| | Bob Moses becomes field secretary in Mississippi for the Student Nonviolent Coordinating Committee (SNCC). |
| **1962** | The Council of Federated Organizations (COFO) is founded to help groups coordinate voter registration in Mississippi. COFO includes CORE, the National Association for the Advancement of Colored People (NAACP), SNCC, and Southern Christian Leadership Conference (SCLC). |
| **1963, June 11:** | President John F. Kennedy delivers a speech on civil rights in which he proposes the Civil Rights Act of 1964. |
| **August 31:** | Mrs. Hamer and a group of seventeen others try to register to vote in Indianola, Mississippi, and are arrested. Mrs. Hamer is forced to leave her home and job. In September, Bob Moses sends Charles McLaurin to find Mrs. Hamer and recruit her to be a field secretary for SNCC. |
| | Throughout the fall COFO begins to plan the Mississippi Freedom Project, which will bring volunteers from across the United States to Mississippi to work in voter registration drives. Bob Moses is made director of the project. |
| **November 22:** | President Kennedy is assassinated and Lyndon B. Johnson becomes president. He pledges to push through the civil rights legislation in Kennedy's memory. |

| 1964, January 23: | The Twenty-fourth Amendment to the United States Constitution is ratified, abolishing the poll tax, which had been used to discourage poor blacks from voting in the South. |
|---|---|
| March: | The Mississippi Democratic Free Party (MFDP) is formed to challenge the all-white Mississippi Democratic Party. |
| June 13: | Freedom Summer volunteers arrive at Western College for Women in Oxford, Ohio, for a week of orientation. |
| June 20–21: | The first group of Freedom Summer volunteers leaves for Missisippi. On June 21, while a second group of volunteers begins orientation, three Freedom Summer workers, Michael Schwerner, James Chaney, and Andrew Goodman, disappear in Neshoba County, Mississippi, after visiting Mount Zion Methodist Church, which had been burned by the Ku Klux Klan. |
| June 23: | The Ford station wagon that the three missing civil rights workers had been driving is found in Bogue Chitto Swamp. |
| June 28: | The second group of Freedom Summer volunteers leaves Oxford for assignments in Mississippi. |
| July 2: | The Civil Rights Act is passed, banning unequal voter registration requirements and racial segregation in public places including schools. |
| Early August: | Bob Moses instructs the Freedom Summer volunteers to focus on signing up Mississippians for the MFDP. |
| August 3: | The bodies of Schwerner, Chaney, and Goodman are found buried at Old Jolly Farm outside of Philadelphia, Mississippi. |
| August 7: | James Chaney is buried in Meridian, Mississippi. |
| August 9: | Funerals for Michael Schwerner and Andrew Goodman are held in New York. |
| August 16: | Freedom School students gather at a conference in Meridian, Mississippi. That evening a memorial service is held for Schwerner, Chaney, and Goodman at the burned-out Mount Zion Methodist Church in Neshoba County. |

| | |
|---|---|
| **August 22:** | The MFDP goes to the Democratic National Convention in Atlantic City and requests to be seated in place of the official state Democratic Party. Mrs. Hamer addresses the Credentials Committee and her testimony is televised nationally. |
| **August 24:** | The Credentials Committee of the national Democratic Party offers a compromise that would allow the MFDP to seat only two delegates. The MFDP votes to turn down the compromise. |
| **September:** | Some Freedom Summer volunteers stay in Mississippi to continue the struggle to empower black people. Twenty-four students including Ben Chaney, brother of the slain civil rights worker James Chaney, attempt to enroll in white schools in Meridian, Mississippi. |
| **October 14:** | Martin Luther King Jr. receives the Nobel Peace Prize for combating racial inequality through nonviolence. |
| **1965, August 6:** | The Voting Rights Act of 1965 is signed into law, making voting discrimination practices illegal. |

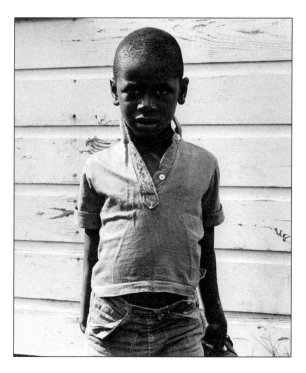

*Ruleville child*

# Appendix A: A Memo to Accepted Summer Project Applicants by Bob Moses

11 June 1964

MEMO TO ACCEPTED APPLICANTS (#3)

To: Mississippi Summer Project Workers
From: Mississippi Summer Project Committee

It has occurred to us that we have perhaps not been forceful enough in impressing upon project workers the importance of alerting the federal government and local officials across the country of our plans for the next few months in Mississippi. The federal government is, we think, aware of the fact that several hundred young people from across the nation will be joing the freedom movement in Mississippi this summer, but awareness is not enough. We must move our government to action. We must insist that some sort of protection be provided for those hundreds of Americans who travel to Mississippi and work here within the grounds of their constitutional rights. We must further insist that the government protect through-out the year citizens who every day are denied their constitutional rights in Mississippi.

On June 8th three white young men visited the city of McComb in south-east Mississippi. They were en route from New Orleans to Jackson, and the purpose of their visit to McComb was to ascertain from the Mayor of the city and from several Negro citizens details concerning preparations for the summer project, both on the part of local officials and the Negro citizenry, with the intention of eventually writing some magazine articles about their experiences. Their appearance in the city was quickly noted, as they drove a car with a Massachusetts tag. Note that the purpose of their visit was purely to gather information, and that they travelled as a disinterested party. At any rate, they were granted a comparatively cordial interview by the mayor of McComb and by some members of the colored community, and then proceeded on their way to Jackson. Just outside of McComb their car was stopped by two carloads of white men and they were badly beaten. They were accused of having visited "nigger town," having talked to "niggers" and having come to McComb to stir up trouble. They were considered by the mayor of McComb to be the "advance guard for the summer invasion."

This incident occurred on June 8th, not a week ago. It is essential that federal officials recognize the nature of the opposition we are faced with, and be prepared to offer the protection the situation demands. To this end we are urging everyone who is planning to come to Mississippi this summer to appeal in every way possible to his senators and representatives and, in addition, to local officials. Wherever possible visits should be made to congressmen. Perhaps your Freedom Center will coordinate an emergency visit. Those volunteers whose route south will take them through Washington D.C. should at all costs make plans to stop and visit their federal representatives. The Washington SNCC office at 3418 11th Street, N.W. will be able to aid you in this direction. You should advise relatives, friends, and all interested parties to continue your appeal once you have left for Mississippi. Telegrams, letters, and all the usual means of appeal should be employed.

We cannot too strongly impress upon you the need for your utmost cooperation in this matter of alerting the nation to the need for federal intervention in Mississippi. Pressure has been applied to federal officials, but it obviously has not been sufficient. We are convinced that if we will continue and reinforce our efforts in this area we can expect results.

Appendix B: Five Pages from a Report Compiled by the
Student Nonviolent Coordinating Committee (SNCC) Detailing
the Results of the Mississippi Freedom Summer Project

DEVELOPMENT OF THE MISSISSIPPI PROJECT

Although the Student Nonviolent Coordinating
Committee has had active projects in thirteen Southern
states, it has achieved its most dynamic success in the
state of Mississippi. A state where individual
political life is non-existent, where the economic condition
of a vast majority of the population is appalling, the
home of white supremacy, Mississippi has become the main
target of SNCC's staff and resources.

In August, 1961, SNCC went into Mississippi under
the leadership of Project Director Robert Moses. Overcoming
violence and hardship, SNCC workers have been able to expand
their activity into all five of Mississippi's Congressional
districts. By fall, 1963, SNCC had joined with other
national organizations and many voting and civic groups in
forming a statewide organization, the Council of Federated
Organizations (COFO) and through COFO conducted a Freedom
Vote campaign in which 80,000 disenfranchised Negroes cast
ballots for a Negro in a mock state-wide campaign.
Literacy projects, and food and clothing drives have
been instituted. But preparation for real democracy calls for
much more comprehensive programs to combat the terrible
cultural and economic deprivation of Negro communities in
Mississippi.

Over 1000 persons combined their talents this past
summer in a massive effort to broaden the base of democracy
in Mississippi. The six primary areas encompassed by
the summer project were; community centers, federal programs
research; the white community project; and the legal project.
Personnel consisted of 100 staff persons from civil rights
organizations, including 76 from SNCC; lawyers, doctors,
ministers, and performing artists in addition to the
large core of volunteers. The following pages offer an
extensive overview of the summer's accomplishments.

DIRECTOR OF MISSISSIPPI SUMMER PROJECT: ROBERT MOSES
DIRECTOR OF COMMUNICATIONS FOR THE PROJECT: FRANCIS MITCHELL


FREEDOM SCHOOLS: Director- Dr. Staughton Lynd

    41 established in 20 communities
    2,165 students
    175 full-time teachers, 40 of them professional

LOCATIONS:

| Community | No Students | Community | No students |
|---|---|---|---|
| Columbus (2 schools) | 60 | Canton (3) | 110 |
| Holly Springs (3) | 155 | Meridan (1) | 150 |
| Ruleville (2) | 50 | Moss Point (1) | 40 |
| McComb (1) | 105 | Holmes County (3) | 105 |
| Carthage (1) | 75 | Greenwood (1) | 60 |
| Laurel (1) | 75 | Vicksburg (1) | 60 |
| Clarksdale (4) | 60 | Rural Madison (3) | 225 |
| Greenville (2) | 35 | Hattiesburg (5) | 675 |
| Shaw (1) | 25 | Biloxi (1) | 35 |


COMMUNITY CENTERS: Director-Miss Annell Ponder (SCLC)

    15 established in 15 communities
    61 full-time workers, including 2 administrative staff

Programs included: Literacy, recreation (art, music, dance)
               day care and health, and libraries.

Locations

| | | |
|---|---|---|
| Greenville | Vicksburg | Canton |
| Ruleville | Greenwood | Batesville |
| Meridan | Shaw | Harmony |
| Clarksdale | Hattiesburg | |
| Mileston | Holly Springs | |

VOTER REGISTRATION AND FREEDOM: Director of Freedom Registration-
                               Dona Moses (SNCC)

    Figures are not available for voter registration
    attempts. However, there were 65,000 freedom
    registration forms.

FEDERAL PROGRAMS RESEARCH: Director-Jesse Morris (SNCC)

    15 workers engaged in research on existent or
    potential federal programs for Mississippi.

## Locations

| | |
|---|---|
| Greenwood | **four volunteers**, research school lunch programs, social security benefits and federally assisted child day care centers. |
| Canton | Five persons research farmers' unions farmers' cooperatives and other programs related to farmers. |
| Itta Bena | One worker researches the development of community center facilities. |
| Jackson | Six researching public health programs, small business goverment assistance, cooperatives and agricultural development programs. |
| Carthage | Three volunteers research farmers' loans and social security benefits. |

WHITE COMMUNITY PROJECT:  Director  Ed Hamlett (SNCC)

25 staff and summer volunteers, mostly southerners, worked in a pilot project in Mississippi white communities.  They were based in Jackson, Greenville, Meridan, Vicksburg, with the bulk in Biloxi.

Their aim:  To bring about some awareness of the rapidity of social change in America, and to find white Mississippians who will work to achieve social change with a minimum of friction.

LEGAL PROJECT:  Coordinator OOR. Hunter Morey (SNCC)

Law Students Project:  15 law students provided by the Law Students Civil Rights Research Council (156 Fifth Avenue, New York City) worked on assigment from COFO to project offices around the state.  They were primarily responsible for gathering data on arrests, collecting evidence on voting discrimination, taking affidavits and contacting federal agencies.  In addition they clerked for lawyers handling COFO cases in various areas.

LEGAL AID: (In connection with summer project, not part of it.)

Lawyers' Constitutional Defense Committee--supplied about 40 volunteer lawyers on a two-week rotating basis through the Jackson Office.  Others through offices in Memphis and New Orleans.

NAACP Legal Defense and Education Fund, Inc.--provides coordination for LCDC program, and handles some cases on their own.

Lawyers' Committee for Civil Rights Under Law ("President's
Committee") Officially represents ministers connected with
the National Council of Churches program.

National Lawyers' Guild Committee for Legal Assistance in
the South--provided 60 volunteer lawyers on a rotating basis.


SUPPLEMENTARY PROGRAMS:

Medical Committee:

    Works on a rotating basis with teams based in
    Clarksdale, Greenwood, Hattiesburg, and Jackson.
    Team usually includes: one physician, one psychiatrist,
    one technician or registered nurse, one dentist.

    Since medical staff are not licensed to practice in
    the state, their work is mainly: giving advice,
    developing rapport with local doctors, arranging with
    local doctors to make immunization available to staff
    and volunteers, in some cases training project staff in
    first aid and home nursing.

NATIONAL COUNCIL OF CHURCHES:

    By the end of the summer nearly 400 ministers had
    participated in a program directed by the National
    Council of Churches' Commission on religion and Race.
    The largest number worked as counselors to volunteers in
    projects around the state. Others worked in addition to
    develop rapport with local clergy, in making visits
    to jails, and to boost northern support.

    In Hattiesburg and Canton, ministers worked on a one-week
    rotating basis adding man-power to the voter registration
    drives. The effort in Hattiesburg has been continuous
    since SNCC conducted the first Freedom Day last January.

FREE SOUTHERN THEATER:

    The theater was first conceived of by three SNCC workers
    last spring. Two of them, Gilbert Moses and John O'Neal,
    are now directors of the theater along with Richard Schecter,
    editor of the Tulane University Drama Review.

    An integrated company of eight persons made a tour of
    thirteen areas throughout the state performing "In White
    America." Performances were free and offered in connection
    with the Freedom Schools.

MISSISSIPPI CARAVAN OF MUSIC:

    Over 25 professional singers and musicians toured
    the state performing and teaching workshops in
    Freedom Schools, community centers and churches, under
    the sponsorship fo the New York Council of Performing
    Artists,. The Project was directed by Bob Cohen.

-5-

    Some artists who have participated in the project thus
    far are: Julius Lester, Len Chandler, Jackie
    Washington, David Segal, Dick Davy and Jim Crockett.


Formal Northern Support for the Mississippi Summer Project and
recruitment of volunteers is organized by SNCC's seven
Northern offices (such as the one in New York City) and
by the 62 friends of SNCC Groups across the nation.

# SOURCE NOTES

Mr. James Williams

Mrs. Williams

P. 1      "All we want . . . America." Watson, *Freedom Summer,* p. 258.

P. 1      "just to have . . . to read." Mills, *This Little Light of Mine,* p. 12.

P. 1      "I had never . . . the Constitution." Fannie Lou Hamer, transcript of interview, University of Southern Mississippi, p. 4.

P. 1      "hateful policemen." Mills, p. 24.

P. 1      "Well, killing . . . with civil rights." Ibid., p. 39.

P. 1      "I am determined . . . Mississippi registered." Ibid., p. 79.

P. 3      "went off to fight for freedom." Mrs. Robert Goodman, in Gillon, "10 Days That Unexpectedly Changed America," p. 226.

P. 3      "I'm scared but I'm going." Watson, p. 83.

P. 3      "This is terrible . . . to vote." Gillon, p. 233.

P. 3      "If someone . . . about this?" Cagin and Dray, *We Are Not Afraid,* p. 243.

PP. 3–4    "We hope . . . around $500." Bob Moses, memo to accepted applicants, USM Archives, mm 108.

P. 5      "The quiet grace . . . to watch." Tracy Sugarman, handwritten log no. 1, p. 2, Mississippi Department of Archives & History.

P. 5      "This is part . . . and yours are one." Cagin and Dray, p. 30.

P. 5      "the Closed Society . . . key is the vote." Belfrage, *Freedom Summer,* p. 10.

P. 5      "race-mixing *trash.*" Watson, p. 32.

PP. 5–6    "No one should . . . back of the house." Ibid., p. 29.

P. 6      "If you don't . . . they're doing." Ibid., p. 30.

P. 6      "You must . . . this summer." Ibid., p. 31.

P. 6      "Your legs, your . . . groin can't." Ibid.

P. 6      "the mob." Ibid., p. 30.

P. 6      "sheepish." Ibid.

P. 7      "I started wearing . . . put in jail." Charles McLaurin, interview with author, January 26, 2013.

P. 7      "fell in love . . . Hamer." McLaurin, "Reflections," p. 23.

P. 7      "for investigation." Sugarman, *We had Sneakers,* p. 23.

P. 7      "was a mess." Sugarman, *Stranger at the Gates,* p. 6.

P. 7      Christopher Wren, "Mississippi, the Attack on Bigotry." *Look* magazine, September 8, 1964, pp. 20–21.

P. 8      "*Look* magazine . . . even bigger." Watson, p. 35.

P. 8      "mixers." Watson, *Freedom Summer,* p. 81.

P. 8      "Goatee" and "Whiskers." Cagin and Dray, p. 12.

P. 8      "building shelves . . . painting." Huie, *Three Lives for Mississippi,* p. 58.

P. 8      "All of us were . . . Queens College." Ibid., p. 90.

P. 9      "scare the Commie . . . to Mississippi." Ibid. p. 83.

P. 9      "Jew-boy with the beard." Ibid., p. 86.

P. 9      "Don't worry. . . . It's safer." Watson, p. 84.

P. 10     "Mickey did all the driving." Andy Schiffrin, phone interview with author, March 6, 2013.

P. 10     "When we hit . . . was a problem." Ibid.

P. 10     "I stayed with the Waterhouse family." Ibid.

P. 10     "Her opening . . . to change it." Fred Bright Winn, e-mail to author, February 1, 2013.

P. 10     "But because . . . months later." Ibid.

P. 11     "Mom, cook up . . . coming over." Cagin and Dray, p. 35.

P. 12     "communication." Ibid., p. 41.

P. 12     "If you're not . . . four-thirty." Huie, p. 97.

P. 12     "Dear Mom and Dad . . . love, Andy." Watson, p. 84.

P. 13     "A tire or . . . be fatal." Huie, p. 97.

P. 14     "and 'investigated.'" Cagin and Dray, p. 7.

P. 15     "I guess . . . my own gun." Huie, p. 102.

P. 15     "for investigation." Watson, p. 79.

P. 15     Mickey . . . was told no. Cagin and Dray, p. 18.

P. 16     "calm and collected." Ibid., p. 45.

P. 16     "Now, let's see . . . County." Ibid., p. 286.

P. 17     "I thought you . . . out of the car." Ibid., p. 292.

P. 17     "Ashes to ashes . . . you stay here." Huie, p. 118.

P. 17     "Save one for me." Cagin and Dray, p. 295.

P. 19     "Well, boys . . . is *dead*!" Huie, p. 121.

P. 21     "I'm just hoping and not thinking." Watson, p. 97.

P. 22     "Our goals . . . a huge job." Belfrage, p. 10.

P. 22     "Yesterday morning . . . no authority." Ibid., p. 11.

P. 22     "The responsibility . . . local police." Watson, p. 36.

P. 23     "Small physically . . . incredibly composed." Martha Honey, interview with the author, August 8, 2012.

P. 23     "I was in awe . . . husband, Mickey." Sugarman, *Sneakers*, p. 23.

P. 23     James Chaney . . . disappeared. Watson, p. 80.

P. 23     "No one . . . to breathe." Belfrage, p. 15.

P. 24     "You all . . . up against." Martha Honey, phone interview with author, August 8, 2012.

P. 24     "Everyone suspects . . . says anything." Barbara, in Martinez, *Letters from Mississippi*, p. 31.

P. 24     Friends of Freedom in Mississippi. Dittmer, *Local People*, p. 239.

P. 24     "there was . . . what to do." Andy Schiffrin, phone interview with author, March 6, 2013.

P. 25     "We searched swamps . . . rural Mississippi." Dittmer, *Local People*, p. 250.

P. 25     "If they're missing . . . stirred up." Cagin and Dray, p. 323.

P. 25     "Those boys . . . embarrass Mississippi." Preston Hughes, phone interview with author, March 4, 2013.

P. 25     "They'll do anything . . . publicity for it." Mars, *Witness in Philadelphia*, p. 85.

P. 25     "a hoax . . . of the nation." Robert Shelton "Klan Wizard Calls Disappearance 'Hoax.'" *The Fiery Cross*, Newspaper of the United Klans of America out of Alabama, July 1964.

P. 26     "I knew the . . . dangerous situation." Mars, p. 87.

P. 26     "the most trusted man in America." Folkenflik, David. "Walter Cronkite, American's 'most trusted man,; Dead." July 18, 2009.

P. 26     "Good evening . . . of Philadelphia." Watson, p. 86.

P. 27     "I can't play . . . around the house." Erenrich, *Freedom Is a Constant Struggle,* p. 328.

P. 27     "As you probably . . . and the FBI.)" Andy Schiffrin, letter to parents, June 23, 1964.

PP. 27–28     "There has been . . . around now." Cagin and Dray, p. 350.

P. 28     "Everyone in . . . out to do." Dickson, "Memories of A Movement," p. 20.

P. 28     "I knew . . . ready for it." Martha Honey, phone interview with author, August 8, 2012.

P. 28     "I'm more determined . . . to be done." Gillon, p. 233.

P. 28     "What really . . . since Sunday." Cagin and Dray, p. 330.

P. 28     "Tell me . . . all right?" Ibid., p. 331.

P. 29     "that they were . . . to Mississippi." Ibid.

P. 29     "I knew then that they were dead." Huie, p. 127.

P. 30     "Virtually all . . . for bodies." Cagin and Dray, p. 342.

P. 30     "They had . . . look convincing." Watson, p. 91.

P. 30     "We don't think . . . they deserved." Mars, p. 87.

P. 31     "You know . . . in this." Watson, p. 96.

P. 31     "I don't believe . . . harm them?" Ibid., p. 90.

P. 31     "I am going . . . happened to them." Ibid., p. 97.

P. 31     "I suggest that . . . gone unnoticed." Cagin and Dray, p. 354.

P. 31     "I want to see . . . a publicity stunt." Ibid., p. 355.

P. 31     "foolhardy." Ibid.

P. 31     "was like a funeral parlor." Watson, p. 100.

P. 31     "It's badly . . . three boys." Belfrage, p. 24.

P. 31     "If you think . . . liberate *you*." Ibid., p. 24.

P. 31     "My dad pleaded . . . back home." Linda Davis, phone interview with author, November 30, 2012.

P. 32     "Suddenly hundreds . . . and determination." Watson, p. 100.

P. 32     "They followed . . . in the place." Belfrage, p. 23.

P. 32     "I wondered . . . obituary photograph." Ibid.

P. 32     "The Search in Mississippi." Watson, p. 100.

P. 32     "Governor Wallace . . . not telling." Ibid, p. 97.

P. 33     "That's the wife . . . men!" Cagin and Dray, p. 356.

P. 33     "I want to . . . husband back." Ibid. p. 357.

P. 34     "I imagine . . . days now." Watson, p. 93.

P. 34     "It usually . . . finish this quilt?" Erenrich, p. 328.

P. 35     "suicide mission." Cagin and Dray, p. 358.

P. 35     "disappearance." Ibid., p. 359.

P. 35     "deputies." Ibid.

P. 35     "What are you . . . all shot!" Ibid., p. 360.

P. 35     "What in . . . doin' here?" Ibid.

P. 35     "I'm not leaving . . . intimidate me." Ibid.

P. 35     "I'm not leaving . . . me killed, too." Ibid.

P. 36     "packed, scared . . . and ready." Belfrage, p. 24.

P. 36     "All of you . . . never turn back." Jim Forman, in Belfrage, p. 25.

P. 36     "The kids are dead." Ibid.

P. 36     "simply 'disappeared.'" Ibid., p. 26.

P. 36     "When we heard . . . Negroes of Mississippi." Ibid.

P. 36     "In our country . . . won't get done." Ibid.

P. 36     "Moses, usually . . . to us." Linda Davis, phone interview with author, November 30, 2012.

P. 37     "invasion." Mars, p. 81.

P. 37     "We're in the . . . squad cars." Linda Davis, postcard dated Sunday, June 28.

P. 38     "Most of us . . . Miss. Border." Anonymous letter marked "Ruleville, July 5." Martinez, p. 46.

P. 38     "Violence hangs . . . dead air." Watson, p. 113.

P. 38     "I felt as strange . . . down the street." Fred Bright Winn, transcript of interview, University of Florida, p. 5.

P. 38     "The first night . . . own safety.'" Len Edwards, interview with author, February 10, 2013.

P. 38     "Watching her . . . to Ruleville." Sugarman, *Sneakers*, p. 24.

P. 39     "never leave." McAdam, p. 258.

P. 39     "the week . . . of harassment." Belfrage, p. 37.

P. 39     "to stir people . . . and trashed." Len Edwards, phone interview with author, February 20, 2013.

P. 39     "reckless walking." Watson, p. 114.

P. 39     YOU ARE IN . . . WITH CAUTION. Belfrage, p. 52.

P. 39     "incidents." Cagin and Dray, p. 386.

P. 39     "All the whites . . . to the boys." Belfrage, p. 39.

P. 39     "The FBI . . . white Southerners." Len Edwards, phone interview with author, February 10, 2013.

P. 39     "ramshackle house." Ibid.

P. 39     "The Highway Patrol . . . but be careful." Ibid.

PP. 39–41     "We were glad . . . along with us." Mrs. Bernice White, transcript of interview, Tougaloo College Archives, pp. 28–29.

P. 41     "[They] press . . . your coming." Anonymous letter marked "Meridian," Martinez, *Letters from Mississippi*, p. 51.

P. 41     "Children and . . . a religious event." Letter from Geoff, marked "Batesville," Martinez, p. 50.

P. 41     "the poor part . . . so energetic." Andy Schiffrin, phone interview with author, March 6, 2013.

P. 41     "The girls are always asking questions." Andy Schiffrin, letter to parents dated June 23, 1964.

P. 41     "Andy is . . . come back again." Letter from Rosalyn Waterhouse to Shirley Schiffrin (Andy's mother), dated July 12, 1964.

P. 42     "It's very generous . . . this way." Sugarman, *Stranger at the Gates*, p. 48.

P. 42     "I'm sorry I . . . come here." Ibid., p. 53.

P. 42     "Mama told us . . . white people." Dr. Eugene Giles, phone interview with author, March 9, 2013.

P. 42     "Before we'd . . . on the windows.'" Ibid.

P. 42     "Mrs. Magruder . . . the movement." John Harris, letter to Mr. Jim Woodrick dated September 20, 2003. Courtesy of Mississippi Department of Archives & History.

P. 43     "And the Freedom . . . want the cat." Dr. Stacy White, phone interview with author, December 3, 2012.

P. 43     "Mom would . . . for years." Dr. Eugene Giles, phone interview with author, March 9, 2013.

PP. 43–44 "Our hostesses . . . are staying." Letter from "Jo" to "John and Cleo" marked "Canton, July 10." Martinez, p. 53.

P. 44     "One family . . . with him." Anonymous letter, n.d., Martinez, p. 53.

P. 45     "We've come . . . that way, Miss." Watson, p. 111.

P. 45     "thousands of men." Cagin and Dray, p. 367.

P. 45     "When the federal . . . in the area." Ibid., p. 368.

P. 45     "In spirit . . . the Klan." Ibid., p. 373.

P. 47     "But we have . . . to the bodies." Huie, p. 134.

P. 47     "You know . . . wanting money?" Ball, *Murder in Mississippi*, p. 64.

P. 47     "Crosses burned . . . from her job." Ibid.

P. 47     "Who would want . . . Mississippi whites?" Cagin and Dray, p. 368.

P. 47     "stifled their fears." Watson, p. 108.

P. 47     "I had been working . . . Library with it." Fred Bright Winn, e-mail to author, January 31, 2013.

PP. 47–78 "Now that was . . . against the building." Fred Bright Winn, e-mail to author, February 1, 2013.

P. 48     "threat of death." Fred Bright Winn, transcript of interview, University of Florida, p. 6.

P. 48     "Dad, I hope . . . a few days." Watson, p. 111.

P. 48     "Many faced real scary stuff." Rita Schwerner Bender, interview with author, November 16, 2012.

P. 48     "There was violence." Mrs. Bernice White, transcript of interview, Tougaloo College Archives, p. 8.

P. 48     "When she . . . when she came." Ibid., p. 23.

P. 48     *"Is this America?* . . . threatened daily?" Watson, p. 249.

P. 48     "They were all . . . fighting for." Andy Schiffrin, phone interview with author, March 6, 2013.

P. 49     "The pressure . . . really intense." Cagin and Dray, p. 375.

P. 49     "He perceived . . . no one was safe." Ibid.

P. 49     "How could you . . . like this?" Ibid., p. 253.

P. 50     "justifiable homicide." Ibid., p. 254.

P. 50     "I have no proof . . . in this." Watson, p. 120.

P. 50     "Never seen them before." Ibid.

P. 50     "close the springs of racial poison." Ibid., p. 121.

P. 51     "Get out . . . Get going!" Ibid., p. 380.

P. 51     "People here . . . starving and afraid." Ibid., p. 122.

P. 52     "These young folk . . . do it togther." Ibid., p. 126.

P. 53     "We open school . . . all hoping." Linda Davis, postcard to family dated "Thurs."

P. 53     "I tutored . . . in reading." Vicki Halper, interview with author, November 17, 2012.

P. 53     "This says Ann . . . fast here." Linda Davis, postcard to parents dated "Tuesday."

P. 53     "incredible energy." Andy Schiffrin, phone interview with author, March 6, 2013.

PP. 53–54 "The Freedom School . . . but they love it." "Gail," letter marked "Meridian, Midsummer," Martinez, p. 111.

P. 54     "The women from . . . to be there." McAdam, *Freedom Summer,* p. 89.

PP. 54–55 "My students are . . . in their school." Anonymous letter marked "Hattiesburg, July 8," Martinez, p.107.

P. 55     "Heidi Dole . . . on the room." Sugarman, *Stranger,* pp. 122–123.

P. 55     "In groups . . . dare to try." Sugarman, *Sneakers,* p. 76.

P. 56     "Was very popular . . . they'd never seen." Alan Reich, email to author, May 5, 2013.

P. 56     "The kids . . . in Ruleville." Ibid., p. 202.

P. 56     "the Monkey." Watson, p. 138.

PP. 56–57 "We're on a . . . to register?" Atwater, "If We Crack Mississippi . . . ," p. 18.

P. 57     "There has not been . . . Mississippi constitution." Len Edwards, letter to "Mom Dad and brothers two," from Ruleville, dated June 26, 1964.

P. 57     "It's going to . . . day by day." Atwater, p. 18.

P. 58     "The ghosts . . . constantly asked." Watson, p. 191.

P. 58     "Did you have . . . hope for the best." Andy Schiffrin, phone interview with a reporter from San Diego, California, July 1964.

P. 58     "'frightened' but . . . in the South." "San Diego Man Tells of Fear in Mississippi," *Los Angeles Times,* June 27, 1964.

P. 58     "Solution, while . . . to be spared." Cagin and Dray, p. 371.

P. 59     "civil rights activities." Ibid., p. 391.

P. 59     "'the place.'" Watson, p. 193.

P. 59     "take over." Cagin and Dray, p. 393.

P. 59     "getting warm." Ibid.

P. 59     "The FBI is . . . to thirty thousand dollars." Ibid., p. 394.

P. 59     "Where are . . . start here." Ibid., p. 397.

P. 60     "the faint . . . clearly discernible." Ibid., p. 398.

P. 60     "We must sing . . . this song." Anonymous letter marked "Meridian, August 4," Martinez, p. 216.

P. 60     "O healing river . . . off our sand." Watson, p. 206.

P. 61     "I think . . . American life." Watson, p. 208.

P. 61     "My boy . . . civil rights worker." Ibid.

P. 63     "I'm gonna kill 'em!" Ibid., p. 212.

P. 63     "I want my brother!" Watson, p. 212.

P. 63    "I have been . . . children involved." Anonymous letter marked "Meridian, August 8," Martinez, p. 218.

P. 65    "I am not . . . tribute. . . ." Anonymous letter marked "Laurel, August 11," Martinez, p. 219.

P. 65    "As I stand . . . who *don't care*." Erenrich, p. 360.

P. 65    "I know what's going . . . and the other people died for?" Ibid., p. 361.

P. 65    "The best thing . . . our rights!" Watson, p. 213.

P. 65    "We want our freedom . . . to stand up." Ibid.

P. 65    "Go down . . . heads up!" Erenrich, p. 363.

P. 65    "Dave finally . . . for so long." Martinez, p. 220.

P. 65    "White thugs." Cagin and Dray, p. 411.

P. 66    "They tried . . . in a way." Martha Honey, phone interview with author, August 8, 2012.

P. 66    "As I was riding . . . all those murders." Anonymous letter marked "Laurel, August 11," Martinez, p. 221.

P. 66    "The tragedy . . . gave their lives." Cagin and Dray, p. 411.

P. 66    "They were not . . . be the last." Ibid., p. 412.

P. 67    "I want everyone . . . be punished." Ibid., p. 406.

P. 67    "I want people . . . like that." Ibid., p. 397.

P. 67    "How could a . . . knowing something?" Martin, "Olen Burrage Dies at 82," p. A18.

P. 67    "The first . . . television bulletin." Cagin and Dray, p. 429.

P. 68    "We could not . . . the information." Ball, p. 81.

P. 68    "substantive results." Watson, p. 210.

P. 68    "Mississippi's Giant Houseparty." Ibid.

P. 69    "The fact is . . . 'own it.'" Green, "Family Southern Style," p. D7.

P. 69    "law-abiding." Watson, p. 224.

P. 69    "We will not . . . our rights." Ibid., p. 224.

P. 69    "Segregation is . . . the races." Ibid., p. 225.

P. 69    "I just can't . . . with that mess." Ibid. p. 116.

P. 69    "I don't have the time." Ibid., p. 227.

P. 70    "I got to think about it." Ibid., p. 176.

P. 70    "I can't sign no paper." Ibid., p. 116.

P. 70    "Been advised not to register." Payne, *I've Got the Light of Freedom*, p. 252.

P. 70    "Satisfied with things as they are." Ibid., p. 252.

P. 70    "Volunteers had to . . . up the riders." Belfrage, p. 186.

P. 70    "Many plantations . . . dead end road." Letter from "Joel" marked "Mileston, August 18, Dear folks," in Martinez, p. 82.

P. 70    "The women were . . . the clothing." Mills, p. 100.

P. 70    "Mrs. Hamer . . . to vote." Linda Davis, interview with author, November 20, 2012.

P. 70    "an electric atmosphere . . . Light of Mine.'" Payne, p. 342.

PP. 70–71    "People were afraid . . . *good* time tonight." Payne, p. 262.

P. 71    "I began to . . . a gospel song." Ibid., p. 147.

P. 71    "Tomorra [sic] we . . . even Indianola." Sugarman, *Stranger*, p. 59.

P. 73    "I was . . . registrar of voters." Sugarman, *Sneakers*, p. 206.

P. 73    "From 1956 to 1963 . . . registered." Mrs. Bernice White, transcript of interview, Tangaloo College, p. 27.

P. 73    "Come back . . . to City Hall." Ibid., p. 24.

P. 73    "Maybe we . . . 'uns in there." Ibid., pp. 26–27.

P. 73    "I was by myself . . . voter's rights." Ibid., p. 27.

P. 74    "And, of course . . . interpret." Ibid., p. 28.

P. 74    "You've got to . . . Sign the book." Ibid.

P. 75    "The voter registration . . . courthouse already." Anonymous letter marked "McComb, August 20," Martinez, p. 88.

P. 75    "I was just . . . brand-new way." Dittmer, p. 253.

P. 75    "Canvassing is . . . a long time." Anonymous letter marked "July 2," Martinez, p. 195.

P. 75    "Three different . . . registering people." Letter from "Bill" marked "August 2," Martinez, p. 207.

P. 75    "going down . . . poor houses." Martha Honey, phone interview with author, August 8, 2012.

P. 76    "People wouldn't come to the door." Ibid.

P. 76    "They were so . . . at the door." Dickson, p. 20.

P. 76    "Come down . . . to vote." Martha Honey, phone interview with author, August 8, 2012.

P. 76    "The police have . . . the same 20." Letter from "Jo" marked "Canton, July 10–16," Martinez, p. 114.

P. 77    "Our community in . . . buzzes with activity." Len Edwards, letter to "Ollie" dated August 7.

P. 77    "Isn't it awful . . . in your face?" Martinez, p. 287.

P. 77    "Segregation will . . . see it gone." Martinez, p. 296.

P. 78    "It was something . . . do a good job." Dittmer, p. 261.

P. 78    "The atmosphere in . . . carry on without us." Martinez, pp. 108 and 110.

P. 81    "It was the . . . all about." Watson, p. 215.

P. 81    "Success? . . . Killed." TK

P. 81    "I want us . . . *Sheriff Rainey!*" Huie, p. 146.

P. 83    "When my child . . . to be in vain." Ibid.

P. 83    "The problem . . . desire to kill." Ibid.

P. 84    "The separation of . . . people of Mississippi." Mills, p. 106.

P. 84    "all Mississippians . . . or polka dot." Cagin and Dray, p. 389.

P. 84    "I'm showing . . . run for office." Testimony before Credentials Committee, August 22, 1964, Americanradioworks.publicradio.org/features/sayitplain/flhamer.html.

PP. 84–85    "I used to go . . . letter will get out." Dr. Eugene Giles, phone interview with author, March 9, 2013.

P. 85    "*Everyone* who . . . convention challenge." Watson, p. 174.

P. 85    "No, there's no danger . . . Here's a brochure" Watson, p. 175.

P. 86    "nerve-wracking experience." Watson, p. 219.

P. 86    "Freedom! . . . freedom!" Ibid.

P. 86    "Sydney and I . . . those cheers." Belafonte, *My Song*, p. 8.

P. 86    "I have been . . . *overflowing* with it." Belafonte, p. 8.

P. 86    "to delirious shouts." Ibid., p. 9.

P. 86    "It was a . . . fully before us." Letter from "Bret" to "Dear Folks," marked "Greenwood, August 17," Martinez, p. 209.

P. 86    "came down to help . . . tradition in the South." Pete Seeger, Oral History, AU 101, September 2, 1979, Mississippi Department of Archives & History.

P. 86    "But surely . . . mass imprisonments." Erenrich p. 229.

P. 86    "White people . . . Afro-American songs." Pete Seeger, AU 101, MDAH.

PP. 87–88 "'Ain't Gonna . . . turn them around." Erenrich, p. 314.

P. 88 "feeling death . . . today I die." Watson, p. 220.

P. 88 "My grandfather would feed him." Dr. Stacy White, phone interview with author, December 3, 2012.

P. 89 "I was afraid but so was everyone." Erenrich, p. 252.

P. 89 "We sang . . . everywhere we went." Ibid.

P. 89 "We been waitin' and waitin'!" Ibid.

P. 89 "She brought . . . our audience." Denise Nicholas quoted in Erenrich, p. 252.

P. 89 "A man came . . . kindest gesture." Ibid., p. 253.

P. 89 "We developed . . . nearly overnight." Ibid.

P. 89 "It is pretty . . . Oh, yes I can." Anonymous letter marked "August 19," Martinez, p. 113.

P. 92 "A number of . . . working with us." Dr. Leslie Burl McLemore, interview with author, January 25, 2013.

P. 92 "It was the . . . first-class citizens." Mills, p. 119.

P. 92 "'Fannie Lou, if you . . . that same night." Zinn and Arnove, *Voices of a People's History of the United States,* p. 404.

P. 93 "They beat me . . . flat blackjack." Williams, *Eyes on the Prize,* p. 242.

P. 93 "All of this . . . *Is this America?*" Mills, p. 121.

P. 94 "We didn't come . . . is tired." Ibid., p. 132.

P. 95 "I made four . . . phony compromise." Anonymous letter marked "August 30," Martinez, p. 256.

P. 95 "All my life . . . sick and tired." Mills, p. 93.

P. 95 "Dear Family . . . can do it." Letter from "Gene" marked "Batesville, August 13," Martinez, p. 260.

P. 95 "the town of death." Martinez, p. 269.

P. 95 "I only know . . . will be changed." Letter from "Tommy" to "Dear Mom and Dad" marked "Philadelphia, October 4," Martinez, p. 270.

P. 96 "The killers . . . uncaught and unindicted." Sugarman, *Sneakers,* p. 108.

P. 96 "get Goatee [Mickey]." Watson, p. 269.

P. 96 "could never convict a preacher." Watson, p. 280, and Ball, p. 132.

P. 97 "There are many . . . stand trial." *Clarion Ledger,* www.pbs.org/newshour/media/clarion/kc _summer.html, p. 2.

P. 97 "You're treating . . . to continue." Dwan, "Widow Recalls Ghosts of '64," www.nytimes.com/ 2005/06/17/national/17civil.html, p. 4.

P. 97 "changed Mississippi forever." Watson, p. 296.

P. 98 "Freedom Schools . . . local communities." Dr. Leslie McLemore, interview with author, January 25, 2013.

P. 98 "I'd never known . . . wanted to say." Sugarman, *Sneakers,* p. 144.

P. 98 "We lived . . . up north." Letter from Lelia Jean Waterhouse to Andy Schiffrin, September 4, 1964, part V.

P. 98 "24 students . . . wish me luck." Ibid., part VI.

P. 98 "I am still . . . office every day." Ibid., part VII.

P. 98 "I miss you . . . come back." Ibid.

P. 98 "Freedom Summer . . . President Obama." Dr. Stacy White, interview with author, January 26, 2013.

P. 98 "one of . . . happened in Mississippi." Williams, p. 249.

P. 98 "There were . . . we would be free." Sugarman, *Stranger,* pp. vii–viii.

P. 99 "We have to . . . rights movement." Rita Schwerner Bender, interview with author, November 16, 2012.

P. 99 "The economic issues are still huge." Linda Davis, phone interview with author, November 30, 2012.

P. 99 "Each generation . . . better prepared." Charles McLaurin, interview with author, January 26, 2013.

P. 99 "Education is . . . a miracle." Mrs. Bernice White, transcript of interview, Tougaloo College, p. 56.

P. 99 "The Movement never stops." Charles McLaurin, interview with author, January 26, 2013.

*Linda Davis in Ruleville with two local girls*

*Ruleville resident and his dog*

# BIBLIOGRAPHY

*Local teens at the community center in Clarksdale, Mississippi*

## Books

Ball, Howard. *Murder in Mississippi: United States* v. *Price and the Struggle for Civil Rights*. Lawrence: University Press of Kansas, 2004.

Belafonte, Harry, with Michael Shnayerson. *My Song*. New York: Vintage Books, 2011.

Belfrage, Sally. *Freedom Summer*. Charlottesville: University Press of Virginia, 1965.

Cagin, Seth, and Philip Dray. *We Are Not Afraid: The Story of Goodman, Schwerner and Chaney and the Civil Rights Campaign for Mississippi*. New York: Nation Books, 2006.

Dittmer, John. *Local People*. Champaign: University of Illinois Press, 1995.

Erenrich, Susie, ed. *Freedom Is a Constant Struggle*. Montgomery, AL: Black Belt Press, 1999.

Huie, William Bradford. *Three Lives for Mississippi*. Jackson: University Press of Mississippi, 2000.

Mars, Florence, with assistance of Lynn Eden. *Witness in Philadelphia*. Baton Rouge: Louisiana State University Press, 1977.

Martinez, Elizabeth, ed. *Letters from Mississippi*. Brookline, MA: Zephyr Press, 2007.

McAdam, Doug. *Freedom Summer*. New York: Oxford University Press, 1988.

Mills, Kay. *This Little Light of Mine: The Life of Fannie Lou Hamer*. Lexington: The University Press of Kentucky, 2007.

Moses, Robert P. *Radical Equations: Civil Rights from Mississippi to the Algebra Project*. Boston: Beacon Press, 2001.

Payne, Charles. *I've Got the Light Of Freedom*. Berkeley: University of California Press, 2007.

Randall, Herbert, photographs, text by Bobs M. Tusa. *Faces of Freedom Summer*. Tuscaloosa: The University of Alabama Press, 2001.

Sugarman, Tracy. *Stranger at the Gates*. New York: Hill and Wang, 1966.

———. *We Had Sneakers They Had Guns*. Syracuse, NY: Syracuse University Press, 2009.

Watson, Bruce. *Freedom Summer*. New York: Penguin Books, 2010.

Williams, Juan. *Eyes on the Prize: America's Civil Rights Years, 1954–1965*. New York: Penguin Books, 1987.

Zinn, Howard, and Anthony Arnove. *Voices of a People's History of the United States*. New York: Seven Stories Press, 2009.

## Fiction

Scattergood, Augusta. *Glory Be*. New York: Scholastic Press, 2012.

## Articles

Atwater, James. "If we can crack Mississippi . . ." *Saturday Evening Post*, July 25–August 1, 1964, p. 15.

Dickson, EJ. "Memories of a Movement." *Oberlin Alumni Magazine*, summer 2012, pp. 15–21 and 42–43.

Dwan, Shaila. "Widow Recalls Ghosts of '64 at Rights Trial." *New York Times*, June 17, 2005.

Green, Penelope. "Family, Southern Style." *New York Times*, August 2, 2012, pp. D1–D7.

Grove, Gene. "Night Ride to the South, A Night Ride to Mississippi." *San Francisco Chronicle*, June 25, 1964.

Lomax, Louis, John Howard Griffin, and Dick Gregory. "Mississippi Eyewitness." Special issue of *Ramparts magazine*.

Martin, Douglas. "Olen Burrage Dies at 82; Linked to Killings in 1964." *New York Times*, March 19, 2013, p. A18.

McLaurin, Charles. "Reflections," *Indianola, Journey: Visitor's Guide 2010–2011*, pp. 20–23.

———. "Civil rights tourism draws student group to Delta." Indianola *Enterprise-Tocsin*, July 1, 2010.

Mitchell, Jerry. "Clues on who got the $30K to solve the Mississippi Burning case." On February 16, 2010 in Justice. http://blogs.clarionledger.com/jmitchell/2010/02/page/2/

"San Diego Man Tells of Fear in Mississippi." *Los Angeles Times*, June 27, 1964.

Wren, Christopher. "Mississippi, The Attack on Bigotry." *Look*, September 8, 1964, pp. 20–21.

## Transcripts of Oral Histories

Hamer, Mrs. Fannie Lou. Neil R. McMillen, interviewer, April 14, 1972. University of Southern Mississippi Center for Oral History & Cultural Heritage.

White, Mrs. Bernice. Kim Lacy Rogers, interviewer, August 21, 1995. The Delta Oral History Project, Tougaloo College Archives.

Winn, Fred Bright. Paul Ortiz, interviewer, August 6, 2004. Samuel Proctor Oral History Program, University of Florida.

## Booklets

Indianola Civil Rights History Driving Tour, February 2008, The Hamer Institute at Jackson State University.

Ruleville Civil Rights Driving Tour, February 2008, The Hamer Institute at Jackson State University.

## Unpublished Papers

Sugarman, Tracy. "The Long Hot Summer," Log no. 1, 1964. Mississippi Department of Archives & History, Jackson.

Letter from John Harris to Mr. Jim Woodrick, Sept. 20, 2003. Department of Archives and History, Jackson, Mississippi.

Five postcards from Linda Davis to her family, summer 1964.

## Films

"Freedom on My Mind." Clarity Films, produced and directed by Connie Field and Marilyn Mulford, 1994.

"Freedom Summer." Firelight Films for *American Experience,* PBS, Stanley Nelson, producer and director, 2014.

## Interviews in person with author

Bender, Rita Schwerner, November 16, 2012.

Halper, Vicki, November 17, 2012.

Kibbee, Margaret, January 24, 25, 2013.

McLaurin, Charles, January 26, 2013.

McLemore, Dr. Leslie, January 24, 2013.

White, Dr. Stacy, January 24, 25, 26, 27, 2013.

## Interviews by phone with author

Davis, Linda, November 30, 2012.

Dickson, EJ, August 2, 2012.

Edwards, Len, February 10, 2013.

Giles, Dr. Eugene, February 7, March 9, 2013.

Honey, Martha, August 4, 8, 2012.

Hughes, Preston, March 4, 2013.

Kibbee, Margaret, January 2013.

McLaurin, Charles, January 19, 2013.

Rinaldi, Matthew, August 5, 2012.

Schiffrin, Andy, March 6, 2013.

Sugarman, Tracy, December 19, 2012.

Whitaker, Mrs. Mable Giles, February 1, 2013.

White, Dr. Stacy, December 3, 2012.

## E-mails to author

Bender, Rita, October 8, 10, November 19, 2012.

Canal, Mel, May 3, 2013.

Cooper, Allen, May 4, 2013.

Davis, Linda, January 4, 10, 11, 2013.

Dickson, EJ, August 1, October 1, 2012.

Edwards, Len, February 8, 14, March 25, May 3, 2013.

Halper, Vicki, August 6, November 3, 17, 2012.

Honey, Martha, July 31, August 4, 2012; April 8, 2013.

Hughes, Preston, February 28, 2013.

Levy, Mark, April 2, 2013.

Reich, Alan, May 1, 5, 2013.

Rinaldi, Matthew, August 6, 7, September 28, October 1, 22, 2012; February 13, 14, 20, 24, 26, 2013.

Schiffrin, Andy, March 18, 19, April 2, 22, 2013.

White, Stacy, January 17, 18, 28, 29, 31, February 2, 11, 12, April 1, 8, May 4, 9, 10, 2013.

Winn, Fred Bright, January 31, February 1, 2013.

*David Kotz (standing on right) in a Freedom School classroom*

# PICTURE CREDITS

*Linda Davis and a local resident, Ruleville.*

# INDEX

*George Winter, a volunteer from Ione, California, and a potential voter in Drew*

Page numbers in *italics* refer to illustrations.